Young at Heart

The likes and life of a teenager with Progeria

Hayley Okines

with Alison Stokes

D0166574

Published by Accent Press Ltd 2014

ISBN 9781783753260

Copyright © **Hayley Okines and Alison Stokes** 2014

The right of **Hayley Okines and Alison Stokes** are to be identified as the author of this work has been asserted by the author in accordance with the Copyright, Designs and Patents Act 1988.

All rights reserved. No part of this book may be reproduced, stored in a retrieval system, or transmitted in any form or by any means, electronic, electrostatic, magnetic tape, mechanical, photocopying, recording or otherwise, without the written permission of the publishers: Accent Press Ltd, Ty Cynon House, Navigation Park, Abercynon, CF45 4SN

Cover Image Jason Fry Photography

Foreword

When I first met Hayley Okines at a Sunshine Foundation Progeria Reunion in America she was two years old. In those early years, we had no real understanding of progeria, but knew that the only way to forge ahead towards treatments and cure was together, as a team.

Hayley was one of the first participants in the research that initiated that forward momentum. She participated in The Progeria Research Foundation programs during those early years. In 2005, when she came to the US National Institutes of Health clinical study, she was a shining star – courageous, cheerful and full of hope. Now I see her when she participates in the Boston Children's Hospital treatment trials and she has grown into an intelligent, beautiful, amazing young woman.

In 2007, Hayley and twenty-seven other children were the first to participate in the first-ever progeria drug trial. She is a pioneer – and one of the reasons that we now have the first treatment for progeria. It has taken the tremendous courage and determination of Hayley, her family and others like them to bring us to this point of progress toward a cure.

Leslie B. Gordon, MD, PhD
Medical Director, The Progeria Research Foundation

Hayley's Dedication

I would like to say a massive thank you to my Mum and Dad for always being there for me.

Mum, you are the world's best chauffeur and potato peeler and I would be lost without the Bank of Mum. And Dad, you are a great photographer and have captured so many of our happy family times. I love you both so much.

Mrs G thanks for putting up with me throughout high school and never telling me to shut up.

Courtney for being the 'biggest loser' and making me laugh even at times when I didn't think I wanted to.

Dr Whincup for being the best doctor ever. Whenever I see you it never feels like a horrible hospital appointment, you are more like a friend. You continue to look after me and explain the medical stuff in ways that are easy to understand and not scary. Thank you for your continuous care.

Hayley xxx

Kerry's Dedication

Thanks to my Mum and Dad for your neverending support and love.

My sister Janie for being my rock: you've been there through my darkest times and the fun times too. You are an enormous help to me and Hayley, both physically and emotionally.

My friend Angela for being there to give me a 'kick up the bum' when I need it.

To the medical teams and scientists in the UK and USA – a massive thank you for keeping us up to date with the trials and new treatments. Your relentless research is helping us to understand and fight progeria.

Tracey Gilbert, aka Mrs G, who took on the role of being a mum to Hayley throughout her high-school years. It made me happy knowing that Hayley had someone to talk to as a friend and confidante. Every day you made sure she was all right and never once broke Hayley's trust.

And last, but no way least, Hayley. You may be a mardy-arsed teenager, but you are the reason I get out of bed in the morning. You give me the strength and focus to keep going through the sad times and the good. Your sarcasm and wit make me laugh every day. You are one special daughter.

Kerry

Introduction

People always ask me what it's like being a teenager with progeria. And I never know what to say because there's nothing to it. I don't think of myself as being a teenager with Hutchinson-Gilford progeria; I'm just a teenager. And this book is all about my life as a teenager. But before you start, here are some things you should know...

About me:

- Just because I'm small, it doesn't mean I am a baby. I am seventeen not seven and would prefer it if people talked to me like an adult.
- People who have seen me on TV say, 'you're so happy. How can you stay positive all the time?' But I'm really not a positive person; I can be negative like most teenagers.
- I hate it when people say I have the body of a 136-year-old because I don't feel different from any other teenager.
- I am in a wheelchair because I can no longer walk on my own. But I am not disabled; I just can't walk on my own.
- I have dreams, ambitions and crushes.
- Progeria doesn't define my life, it just makes it more awkward and interesting.

Some things you should know about Hutchinson-Gilford progeria:

- It's a really rare syndrome that makes you age eight times faster than 'normal' and really small.
- There are ninety-four cases in the world, so far, and most people with it die from strokes and heart attacks.
- It's caused by a bad gene.
- It's not catching, it's not passed on in families, it's just bad luck.
- When I first had it, doctors said I probably would't live to see my thirteenth birthday. I've just turned seventeen.

Chapter 1

'Why Am I Such A Rubbish Teenager?'

My thoughts on drugs, dates and getting drunk

I want to let you in on a secret. I really am a sad excuse for a teenager. I may be seventeen but sometimes I feel like I really *am* eight times older. I don't do any of the things that girls of my age are expected to do like drink, smoke, swear or hang around in parks or on street corners. I hate alcohol: wine is horrible and beer smells like old socks. I'd much prefer a cup of tea or a mug of hot chocolate. I never intend to get drunk in my life because drunken people irritate me so much. Smoking is disgusting. My mum smokes and I hate the smell. I don't even swear, well at least not out loud, I just mutter swear words in my head.

I only have one close friend now and her name is Courtney. We first met at primary school when we were four years old and have stayed friends ever since. She has stuck by me through all the horrible times and looked out for me at school. I have thousands of followers on Twitter and friends on Facebook but they are mostly people who have seen me in the TV documentaries, which have been shown all over the world. I have had film cameras following me and filming my life since I was four years old, but I still find it weird when strangers come up to me and say 'Haven't I seen you on TV?' Usually I nod and say, 'Probably.' The last documentary I made was in 2010. I stopped because I didn't like being the centre of attention, but those old programmes are still being shown on different channels like Channel 5 in Britain and the National Geographic Channel in America. I don't like watching them because I look like a baby.

I never stay out late, because I hardly ever go out on my own. Generally I would rather stay at home snuggled under a blanket on the sofa, dressed in my onesie with a cup of tea in one hand, a biscuit in the other, and watch TV, listen to music or read a book. I need to wrap up to keep warm because my body doesn't have the same layer of fat as most people's so I feel the cold. I feel cold even in the middle of summer.

I take drugs, a lot! But don't panic, they are all legal. Since the age of nine I have been part of a pioneering drug trial in America, so I have to take a cocktail of pills every day. Some are because of the trial to find a 'cure' for Progeria and others are to keep my heart healthy – but I'll explain more about the medical stuff later. Mum says I take so many pills I rattle.

Most other girls my age have boyfriends. I don't, although there is a boy who used to be at school that I liked. I'm not going to say his name but I've liked him for a long time. We used to be friends a couple of years ago. Once when we were in maths class he spoke to me. I'm sure I went red. I whispered to Courtney, 'I think I'm going to be sick', which is not very cool. Then, when I dislocated my hips and stopped going to school, I didn't see him for nearly a year. When I went back, he didn't notice me anymore.

Mum used to tease me and say Harry was my boyfriend. Harry Crowther is just a friend who also has Progeria. He lives in Yorkshire, which is the other end of the country from where I live in Bexhill, but we kept in touch on Facebook and both our mums are friends. He's fifteen and has atypical Progeria. It's a different form of the disease from my Hutchinson-Gilford Progeria so he only ages five times faster than normal compared to my eight times. That makes him seventy-five. 'Harry's your toy boy,' Mum says, when she really wants to annoy me. I first met Harry when Mum and I appeared on the TV programme *This Morning*. He's two years older than my brother Louis and likes the same things: computer games and video games. Harry is a real gentleman, he's funny and kind, but he's not my type. My type is more like Nathan Sykes from my favourite band, The Wanted.

Like many teenage girls I have real issues with my body. I don't like any part of me. My knees are knobbly and my arms are really thin. I hate showing them, so I always cover them up with jogging bottoms, hoodies and cardigans. Even my nails are not like proper fingernails, they are just little things on the end of my fingers. I don't agree with plastic surgery but I wouldn't mind being put to sleep if I could wake up with fingernail implants. I always wear a bandana on my head; I feel naked without one. To me it's like going out without underwear. I have a pink one and a white one, which I decorate with a daisy chain. I also have a black one, which I used to wear to match my school uniform. I wear bandanas to cover the fact I have no hair. In my old baby photos I have a thick mop of hair and shiny, fat, pink cheeks. Dad says when I was born it looked like I had highlights. But by the time I was three all my hair had fallen out. I remember, when I started primary school, someone asked me what I would wish for if I had a wish. I said 'nits' because other kids who had hair got nits but I didn't.

When I was twelve or thirteen I went through a phase of wearing a wig. It was dark blonde, shoulder-length with a fringe, the same colour as the hair I used to have. I liked wearing it; it made me feel like the other girls. I could shake my head and my hair would flick around. If I had to choose a favourite part of my body it would be my eyes. When I was born Mum said I had eyes as big as a bush baby's. People tell me I have beautiful blue eyes, but quite frankly I don't see it.

Shopping for clothes is no longer the problem it used to be. When I was ten my body was the size of a two-to-three-year-old, so I could never find clothes to wear that didn't make me look like a baby. Mum had her work cut out sewing clothes I liked to make them fit. I am still only the height of a seven-or-eight- year-old, but at least you can buy fashionable clothes for kids these days. I'm actually smaller than my sister Ruby and she's nine. My biggest problem is finding trousers to fit, because I have a tiny waist and really long legs. That's why most of the time I wear jogging bottoms with elasticated waistbands made of soft fabric. The last time I wore a pair of jeans I got an open sore on my waist where the denim had rubbed my skin. It took ages to heal. I think my feet have stopped growing at size ten, which is OK as I mostly wear Converse trainers.

I guess you could call me anti-social – that's the teenage part of me. I'm addicted to my phone, but not in a stereotypical teenager way. I use it to text Courtney all the time and sometimes I will text Mum and Dad but I don't sit at the dinner table glued to my phone.

And I don't play with it when people are talking to me. I can't stand people who do that. It's really rude and irritating.

Now that I've grown-up I think Mum finds it hard to know what to do. When I was little we did so much together. She took me on some amazing holidays. We went to Florida and Egypt. I also got to meet lots of famous people like Kylie Minogue, Prince Charles, Simon Cowell, Justin Bieber and Steve Irwin the Crocodile Hunter. But now I am seventeen and in a wheelchair I just like staying at home.

Mum says she can't remember being as spoilt as me when she was my age. 'I was a nice teenager,' she says whenever we argue. But Nanna has a different story to tell. She says Mum was a 'bloody nightmare' at my age. She started smoking and drinking at fifteen. And when she was my age she used to go out to discos with her sister Janie. One night, Auntie Janie told me, Mum was so drunk she had to carry her home and when they got to the corner of the street where my nanna lives, she had to sober her up quickly so my nanna wouldn't shout at them. At least I'm never going to be able to get into such a state that I have to be carried home because I'm so drunk I can't walk!

So you see I'm really not a very good teenager.

Chapter 2

'Why Are Parents So Annoying?'

Meet my family

My family is bunch of weirdos, but weird in a good way. I live in a red-brick semi on an estate in Bexhill-on-Sea with Mum, my brother Louis, sister Ruby, three dogs and a cat. Our house has a neat little garden at the front and a big lawn and decking at the back. I also have another brother, Luke, and three sisters, Charlotte, Stacey and Oceana. They don't live with me, but I love them just the same.

Mum and Dad are divorced now, but they are like best friends, which is a good thing. Dad has a flat of his own near the beach in Bexhill, which is a ten-minute drive from our house. We kids stay with Dad every other weekend or a couple of times in the week. Sometimes Dad sleeps over at our house, mostly if Mum goes to visit her sister Janie.

I'm glad that they have sorted their differences as they went through a bad time before the divorce. They were always arguing and saying nasty things to each other. They couldn't even look at each other or talk to each other without having an argument and mostly it would start over nothing. Dad would say Mum was a bad mother which would make her really mad and she would shout back at him. Then Dad would shout louder and Mum would raise her voice.

They would mostly argue when we were in a different room and didn't think we were listening. But it was impossible not to listen as they would be so shouting so loudly. Sometimes Louis, Ruby and I didn't know where to look or what to do. I'm sure the people living in the next street could hear them too. The trouble is they are both opinionated. At first I felt sad and a little bit guilty, because they had only been married for five years and I had wanted them to get married in the first place so that I could be Mum's bridesmaid. When I asked my dad why they always argued, he said, 'We just stopped liking each other', which is really sad.

I have a typical teenage daughter's relationship with my mum. Sometimes we'll shout and say horrible things to each other. Then we'll be upset and say, 'I'm sorry, I never meant the things I said,' and we'll be nice to each other again. Mornings are always the time when we argue the most, especially when I get up and find she's moved my things and I can't find anything. A typical morning goes like this:

Me: 'Where have you put my laptop charger?'

Mum: 'I haven't touched it.'

Me: 'Well I left it on the coffee table last night before I went to bed.'

Mum: 'Well I haven't seen it.'

Me: 'You're the only one who has been in the house.'

Mum: 'Is this it?'

And she'll get it out of the cupboard when I know for a fact I didn't put it there.

One time I was really annoyed with her because we'd run out of sugar. It sounds like a petty thing, but I was getting ready for school and I went into the kitchen to make a cup of tea. That may not seem like a big deal, but believe me it takes a lot of effort to manoeuvre my wheelchair down the hall and into the kitchen without taking the wallpaper off the walls. Then when I poured the tea into my cup, I reached over for the sugar jar and found it was empty, so I had to use icing sugar instead. It was disgusting.

When Mum does things that annoy me, I text Courtney 'I'm so mad' and she'll text me back 'I'm so mad'. It's so weird it usually happens at the same time. Then we'll send each other a picture of our favourite bands and that always cheers us up. Courtney and her mum don't argue as often and me and Mum. Whenever I think bad things about Mum, I always feel bad afterwards but we never say sorry. We just start talking again but never really apologise. I'm not good at apologising.

Sometimes when Mum is in a bad mood or unhappy it's

because she has argued with her friends on Facebook. I don't go on Facebook but Mum is always on there. She has thousands of friends but there are some people who irritate her. Once there was a woman she used to be friends with who started saying horrible things about her, and Mum was really upset. One weekend when Dad took us out for the day Mum went out with her. I was thinking, 'What are you doing? I thought I banned you from seeing her, but I saw you talking to her in the street. Can you just not talk to her?' At times I feel like I'm the adult. I wanted to ground her for a week, lock her in her room and confiscate her phone so that she couldn't go on Facebook; I thought that might make her happy.

Mum says that we kids have no respect for her. I do respect her, it's just I'm just not very good at showing it. I know it can be hard for her because of my progeria. She has taken care of me all my life, looking after me, taking me on all the hospital trips and stuff. She always acts so strong but sometimes I know that she isn't OK. She tries not to let me, Louis and Ruby know, but I know. She doesn't know I know, but I do. When that happens I never know what to say, I'm not good at comforting people. Usually I will tell Ruby to go and give Mum a hug and that seems to help.

My dad is the brains in our family. He's really technical and knows all sorts of weird and clever stuff. Anything to do with gadgets and computers and fixing stuff, he's the man. He knows loads about history and how things are made. He takes us on days out to see art exhibitions or visit museums and parks or for walks along the sea front. Sometimes he annoys me in different ways from Mum, but I still love him. Depending what mood he's in, he can be really irritating, especially when we are sitting together on the sofa watching TV and he starts poking and tickling me. He mostly does it because I'm an easy target and I can't run away. I either find it hilarious or just tell him to stop, depending what mood I'm in.

My sister Ruby is nine years old and is much taller than me. Mum calls her Booby because she's the baby of the family. I was seven when she was born and I really wanted a little sister to play games with and put make-up on. Before she was born I used to put my hands on Mum's pregnant belly and feel her moving inside. When Ruby is in a nice mood, she is the sweetest kid ever. She'll happily run errands for me like going to the shop to buy me chocolate. But when she's in a bad mood she is so horrible. Honestly, she is like nine going on nineteen. She can have such an attitude. I can't really talk much because I have a bad attitude too but I'm the oldest so it's OK for me to be moody and a bit hypocritical. When Ruby is in a bad mood she will start arguing with me for no reason. We are both argumentative people and fight over normal sister things. For example, I will ask her to go upstairs to my bedroom to fetch my headphones or go into the kitchen to fetch me a drink of water or something. And she'll say 'Why can't you do it?'

Then I'll say, 'Do you realise how long it'll take me?' I have to drive my wheelchair out through the living room, making sure there's nothing in the way, to get into my lift and go upstairs. Then when I get to my room I have to get my chair out of the lift and send the lift back down so I have enough room to move my chair around the room, get what I want, call the lift back up, get in and go back down. When I've done all that it will take ten minutes.

'It will only take you ten seconds,' I say.

'You can't be bothered to do anything round here,' she says.

And I say, 'That's because I can't!'

Then Mum chips in and says, 'You need to be stop being so horrible to Ruby because she does everything for you.'

And I say, 'She doesn't – only when she's in a good mood.'

I really wish I could just get up and do things for myself, it gets really frustrating. I wish I could do simple things like looking for the remote control for the TV when I want to change channels or walk into the kitchen and get tomato ketchup from the cupboard to put on my dinner. Whenever we argue, Ruby will always try to get last word and I'll shout back, then we both get shouted at by Mum. If the fights get really out of hand Louis will step in and drag Ruby off or slap her, then Ruby cries and Mum gets really mad. When that happens we both know it's time to stop.

The rest of my family know when I'm in a really bad mood; I don't shout, I go completely silent and stick my headphones in my ears and listen to music. Sometimes I crash into the walls with my wheelchair but not on purpose. If I wasn't in the chair I would probably just stomp off and slam the door. Whenever I'm in a bad mood I text my friend Courtney and that always makes me feel better.

Ruby's fashion sense is 'different' to say the least. Courtney's sister is the same age and she has pretty good fashion sense, but Mum still picks Ruby's clothes for her. Once when Courtney was sleeping over at our house, Ruby came downstairs in a short skirt, no tights and a bright yellow spotty top. It was so embarrassing. Half of her tights have holes in them.

Mum is always telling me not to be so nasty to Ruby. 'You used to look the same when you were her age,' she says. But I have photos and hours of TV documentary films that prove I never dressed that badly. Sometimes I wonder why Mum takes her side because she's always moaning at her about the state of her bedroom. It's disgusting and messy and you can't even see the floor. Mum has refused to go in there and clean it. 'Things will start crawling out of there soon,' she says.

Lately Ruby has started to wear make-up but I think she should stop. The other day she came in with dark rings around her eyes. I said, 'Are you wearing make-up?'

'It's only a bit of mascara,' she said.

I told her to take it off. She's only nine, she shouldn't be wearing make-up. When I was her age I used to wear kids' make up but not for real. Once, when she was little, she got hold of Mum's make-up and put eye shadow and mascara all around her eyes – and on the carpet. I laughed a lot but Mum didn't think it was funny.

Whenever I ask her if I can put make-up on her up she looks scared. I don't know why, she used to let me do it when she was younger. It's not as if I hurt her. Well that's not actually true. Once I was curling her hair and I burnt her ear with the irons, but it wasn't my fault. I asked her to sit still but she kept moving. I said sorry but it was awful, she started crying and had a red mark on her ear. I felt really bad. I said 'Sorry, but please don't move next time.' Actually, there wasn't a next time! I think Ruby was relieved when I gave up hairdressing in school!

Despite our fights Ruby knows that whenever she is sad, she can talk to her big sister. She gets sad a lot, mostly thinking about Maddie. Maddie was my best friend. She was three years older than me and had progeria too. She was only eleven when she passed away. It's weird because Ruby was only a baby when it happened but she remembers lots about her. I can't remember

9

things that I did when I was a baby but Ruby talks about the times we would visit Maddie and her family and play on a trampoline with her sisters. I can always tell when Ruby is feeling down because she stays in her room and writes poems. When she is in one of those moods, she will say things like 'I miss Maddie so much.' I tell her that I miss her too.

'She was my best friend,' I'll say. Then I'll talk about our friendship. 'We were so close people used to think we were sisters,' I say.

We only ever argued once – and that was the night before she passed away when she wanted to play my Nintendo DS and I wanted her to play with our Barbie dolls.

'Maddie wouldn't want you to be sad,' I say and that usually makes Ruby feel better. Then we'll talk about all the happy times we shared. I feel it is my duty to cheer Ruby up when she is sad.

My brother Louis is almost a teenager, so he can have a really bad attitude too. He says he doesn't mind helping me around the house, but whenever I ask him to do something he will say 'no' or if he does help he will moan, 'I have to do everything round here.' But he doesn't really do anything except stay in his bedroom or what Mum calls his 'man cave' watching YouTube or playing football games on his X-Box.

Louis is into football and he's quite good at it. He's always kicking his ball around the garden. Mum shouts at him when he scores a goal by knocking her plant pots over. He was hoping to try out for our local football team, Bexhill United, but he developed Osgood-Schlatter disease. He could barely walk on his leg when he first did it, bless him. If he plays football he gets a swelling and pain below his knee. Mum says it's common in boys his age who play sports and is all to do with ligaments and cartilage. So he's been told he can't play aggressive sport, which is bad news for him, but good news for Mum's garden fence.

Louis supports Chelsea Football Club like Dad. Dad has followed Chelsea since he was Louis's age and always goes up to London to watch them play. He takes Louis or Ruby with him and they love it. I don't bother going any more because it's too difficult taking my wheelchair on the Tube in London. And anyway I'm not bothered; I'd rather watch bands than football.

When I was younger I was a team mascot for Chelsea at one of their Champions League matches. We arrived at their stadium, Stamford Bridge, in a limousine with tinted windows and were mobbed by fans who thought we were one of the famous footballers. They must have been so disappointed when we got out of the car. The captain, John Terry, introduced us to all the team. Kylie Minogue, who was my favourite pop star at the time, was also there watching the match. I got to walk out on the pitch in front of 39,000 people with John Terry and Dad. It was special, but really I think Dad enjoyed it more than me.

Louis goes to the same school as me, Bexhill High. When he first started at the big school, he was scared because he didn't know many people. I know exactly how he felt; I was the same when I started high school. I was really tiny and everyone seemed really big. The yard was ginormous and I was always afraid that I would get knocked over by the boys playing football, so my friends would protect me. When Louis moved up to high school, I used to look out for him. He would come and talk to me during the break and lunchtimes and other kids would ask, 'Is Hayley your sister? She is so cute.' He says it's like having a celebrity for a sister.

Whenever I get sick Louis gets really concerned and wishes he could do something to make me better, which is sweet. If I don't feel well, he comes and sits in my room and cheers me up with his silly voices and funny faces. Lately Louis has started taking an interest in the way he looks. He had his hair cut into a quiff, the same as every other male in the population. He looks more grown-up now and does his hair every morning before school. I'm trying to get him to grow his quiff really big like the lead singer from one of my favourite bands, 5 Seconds of Summer.

It's funny because I remember being a bit obsessed with Louis' hair when he was born. I was only four and a half when Dad took me to see him and Mum in hospital. His head was covered in jet-black hair, which I liked to stroke. The other day I caught him standing in front of the mirror in the hall, gelling his hair. I asked him what he was doing. He said 'I'm doing my hair because the wind messed it up.' He is such a girl, but in a good way. It was a proud big sister moment to know that he was taking so much care about his hair. He is such a hipster.

I have another brother and sister, too, Luke and Oceana. They are not my actual brother and sister like Ruby and Louis. Their mother Jane used to be married to my dad before he met my mum. Actually it was Dad's ex-wife Jane who introduced Mum and Dad as they used to go out in a group when they worked together at a supermarket. Now Jane is remarried and Oceana and Luke are their children. Oceana is twelve and has her own bunch of friends, so I don't see her that often, but Luke comes to visit us a lot. Before I was born Mum and Dad used to babysit him so he would often sleep over at our house. Luke is massively ginger and girls like him. He is quite fit, but I can't see it because he's my brother and that would just be wrong. He belongs to Gillingham Jumpers, a trampoline club. He is good at it, too. He entered the TV show *Britain's Got Talent* and made it through to the second round until he dislocated his knee and couldn't go, which was not good. I think Luke looks funny. He is really tiny, not much taller than Louis. But he has really broad shoulders, really long arms and really small legs. His body looks like a triangle, it's hilarious. He's hoping to make Team GB for the 2016 Olympics in Brazil. I hope he does, it would be so cool if he won a gold medal and I could say my brother is an Olympic champion.

Recently I've become an auntie. Charlotte is my oldest sister, I call her my sister but actually she and her sister, Stacey, are my half-sisters. Their mum Jane was my dad's first wife. Charlotte is thirteen years older than me and Stacey is seven years older. They used to have a baby sister, Lucy, but she died of cot death when she was eight weeks old, so I never got to meet her. Charlotte and Stacey used to live with us when I was little. Charlotte used to take me down the park and show me off to her friends. They would make a fuss of me cooing and saying things like 'she's so cute', which is funny because that's what I now say about my nephew. Babies have that effect on me.

When Charlotte first told us that she was having a baby, I was so excited. Dad and I went to the hospital with her when she had her scan; it made a change to watch someone else being prodded and poked as it's usually me. The nurse smeared some jelly stuff over Charlotte's baby bump and ran a machine over her belly. Then this black-and-white blob thing appeared on the screen.

Charlotte and the nurse were so excited. 'It looks like you have a healthy baby boy,' the nurse said. I was grinning, even though it was hard to see how she could tell. But then she pointed at this little thing sticking out on the scan and it sort of made sense.

At this point I should tell you that I already had a niece and nephew but Stacey is their mum and I wasn't as close to her when they were born, so I didn't feel like I was such a big part of their lives. When Charlotte gave me a photo of my new nephew taken at the scan I felt really special and I thought I had better get my act together and start doing auntie things. So Mum, Dad and I hit the shops. We bought a wicker basket and started filling it with the sort of things I thought Charlotte and her baby would like. I chose a sweet Ralph Lauren shirt. It was like a proper man's cotton shirt, but really tiny, with a little collar, buttons down the front and a teeny Ralph Lauren logo on the front. 'He is going to be such a hipster,' I said to Mum as I added it to our baby hamper.

I was actually in the middle of a lesson in school when Charlotte gave birth. The teacher was talking to the class about something, I can't even remember what, when I got a text from Mum. It said, 'Hello, Auntie Hayley. Charlotte had her baby at twelve.' I almost screamed as I was so excited. 'Goodness, my sister has had her baby,' I said.

Two days after my nephew was born and Charlotte was allowed to take him home, we went to visit them. He was so cute – with a mass of hair just like Louis when he was born.

'He looks Chinese,' I said to Charlotte and she laughed.

We gave her the baby hamper and she loved the little Ralph Lauren shirt.

'You have really good taste in clothes,' she said to me and I felt really proud.

Charlotte and her husband John decided to call the new baby Loydd, spelt with one L and two Ds, which is an odd way to spell it, I think. At first I thought Loydd was tiny, but when Charlotte asked me if I would like to hold him and placed him on my lap I realised he was ginormous. He was really long, almost as big as me. Both Charlotte and her husband John are tall, so that's to be expected. I think he liked me because when I said 'Hello, Loydd' he looked like he was laughing. I noticed he had a mark on his head.

'What's that?' I asked.

Charlotte explained it was a birthmark and it might fade when he was older.

'It looks like the rock sign with two horns sticking out' I said. 'That is so cool; he's going to be a rock 'n' roll baby!'

I have nicknamed him Squidge because he is just so chubby and ... squidgy. He's a big baby; he was 9lb 12oz when he was born, which Mum tells me is really big for a baby. I was only 6lb 6oz.

Charlotte makes such a good mother. She is always taking selfies of her and Loydd together and sending them to my phone. She talks to him all the time and makes him laugh a lot. When he gurgles and makes those funny noises that baby's make Charlotte says, 'Yeah, I know. It's so hard. Tell me more.' That always makes Loydd laugh even more. She talks to him like he's a real grown-up person, which is so funny and a little bit embarrassing. Once she was standing at the supermarket check-out chattering away to him and a woman in front thought she was talking to her.

It's nice to visit Charlotte and play with Loydd, but I wouldn't want babies of my own. Loydd is cute but I know they don't stay like that. They will grow up to be like Louis and Ruby and they have put me off having children for good.

Chapter 3

'Angel Is So Gross But I Love Her'

Let me introduce you to my pets

In our house we have three dogs and a ginger cat. Angel is the oldest. She is a Shih Tzu and is meant to be cream-coloured but quite often she's black, especially when she had been digging in the garden. She has a long, matted beard, which seems to be a magnet for her food. It's gross. She stinks and is disgusting but I love her all the same. But I don't let her lick me: that's gross.

Angel was my first dog: Mum bought her for me as a Christmas present when I was thirteen. I named her Angel because Mum says that I am her angel. She follows me everywhere and sits on the back of my wheelchair and sleeps on my bed at night. She is the best dog ever; she's never naughty. When we go out walking, I hold Angel's lead in one hand and drive my wheelchair with the other. Sometimes she will walk around a pole and I have to reverse my chair backwards. Angel is a real 'people dog'. Old people love to stop and talk to her and Angel likes it when a fuss is made of her. I would like to train her as therapy dog and visit people in hospitals and old people's homes. It would be nice for the people in hospitals because dogs make people happy. But I would have to bath her every day.

We also have two teacup Chihuahua puppies called Mollie and Dollie. They are Boo's pups. Boo was my dog. I had always wanted a Chihuahua because they are tiny and cute, so Mum bought her as a present for my fifteenth birthday. She was only eight weeks old when I first had her. She was really small and really cute with big ears like a Gremlin from the films. She would curl up on a blanket on my lap and fall asleep while I was stroking her, then wake up and lick my fingers. It was really sweet. Our cat Tango would stare at her, I'm sure she thought Boo was a rat or something.

When Boo grew up, she used to follow me everywhere. She would snuggle up on my shoulder whenever I was lying on the sofa watching TV and she would sit on the back of my wheelchair and ride around the house with me. At night she would sleep on the bottom of my bed. She was like my best friend. I say was, because a really horrible thing happened to my Boo.

When she was two I thought it would be really sweet if Boo had puppies so I asked Mum.

'I don't think so,' Mum said. 'She's so tiny she might have trouble having pups.'

'Please,' I begged. 'Just think how cute it would be to have puppies around the house? And Boo would make such a good mother.'

'I know. But once I see those pups, I won't be able to part with them.'

'Boo wants to have babies. Don't you, Boo?' I said. Boo looked up at me with her big chocolate-drop eyes and wagged her tail.

'See. She's saying yes.'

So I won and Mum, against her better judgement, found a doggy boyfriend for Boo. It was really strange seeing Boo pregnant. She was so small and she had this big, round belly. We were all excited. Mum went out and bought a special dog crate and soft fluffy bedding ready for Boo to have her pups and she watched videos of dogs having puppies, so she knew what to do when Boo went into labour. Over the next eight weeks Boo grew so big she could hardly walk. I felt so sorry for her, she looked so awkward.

A couple of days before my sixteenth birthday Mum told us she thought Boo was going to have her puppies soon because she had started nesting. I thought only birds did that, but Mum explained that Boo had started digging the blankets on her bed trying to make a nest. I was so excited I asked Mum if I could stay home from school to help when the puppies arrived. Ruby and Louis went to school and Mum and I waited for the puppies to be born.

Suddenly Mum noticed two little feet sticking out of Boo's bottom end and started to panic a little bit. She rang a friend who breeds dogs and knew what to do. She told Mum to try to pull the puppy out gently. But by the time she did that the puppy was cold and dead. Poor Mum, she tried to rub it in a towel and breathe on it to get it breathing, but it was no use, the puppy had died. Poor Boo, she was trying really hard to have her puppies, but she was really struggling.

After about eight hours, Mum took Boo to the vets and they kept her in and gave her a Caesarean section to get the puppies out. An hour later the vet rang to say Boo was ready to come home. She had four puppies, but one had died. It was so exciting to see the puppies. They didn't even look like dogs, their eyes were closed and their fur was all velvety and soft. Boo looked exhausted, she just lay in her new bed, feeding her puppies and letting us stroke them. Mum was still worried about Boo because she wasn't walking around or eating. She gave her water from a syringe and let her lick honey off her finger. Over the next couple of days, Boo was still not eating and had started being sick, so Mum took her and the pups to the emergency vet.

A couple of hours later she came home and I could see had been crying.

'Boo had an infection. The vet injected her with adrenalin and tried to massage her heart but she passed away,' Mum cried. 'It was horrible. I held her and told her we loved her.'

It was awful. Mum was crying and saying, 'It's all my fault; I should never have let Boo have puppies.' It was near Christmas and was supposed to be a nice happy time and it all went wrong. It was worse than a human dying. It was a good thing we still had the pups and had to look after them and feed them, that made it a bit easier.

After Boo died, I felt sad for Angel. They shared a basket and always slept together. When Boo didn't come home from the vet's, Angel just lay in her basket looking for her friend. She looked so sad and lonely. At night Angel sleeps in Boo's space at the bottom of my bed. Sometimes she wakes up in the middle of the night and starts barking at the wall. It kind of creeps me out. She just sits there, growling at nothing. I wonder if she sees Boo. I always think of Boo, so maybe Angel does too. Sometimes, when Angel is barking at nothing in particular, Ruby says, 'It's OK, she's only talking to Boo.' That's the cutest thing ever. It's nice that she thinks of Boo like that.

Only two of the pups survived and Mum decided that after everything that had happened we couldn't part with them too. She named them Dollie and Mollie – both are spelt with 'ie' not 'y', which is strange I think. I hate the name Mollie; I wanted to call the pups some really awesome names. When she was first born she was a really dark colour so I suggested we should call her Coco. I wanted to call Dollie 'Bambi' because she looked exactly like Boo did when she was a puppy when her legs were all wobbly when she walked and she looked like Bambi in the film. Mum said, 'Bambi is a deer's name. You can't call her after a deer.' So she named her after person instead! I hate it when people give dogs human names. You wouldn't call a baby Patch so why call a puppy by a person's name? Dollie is the smallest and was the runt of the litter but she's definitely the boss. She pins Mollie down when they are play-fighting.

One time I was going out into the hall in my wheelchair and Mollie was running in front of my wheels, wagging her tail all excited. Suddenly I felt a bump. Mollie squealed and ran behind the sofa. My wheelchair had run over her foot. My heart thumped. I was so scared I didn't know what to do. I couldn't move and I couldn't go to help her. I just sat in my chair, crying. Mum was in the kitchen at the end of the hallway and heard Mollie cry. She shouted, 'I'll wrap that wheelchair around your neck.'

That made me cry even more. 'I didn't mean to do it, she just ran under my wheels,' I sobbed.

When Mollie ventured out from behind the sofa she was limping, I felt even guiltier. Mum took her to the vet and she came back with her leg in a splint and a bill for £197. But she hasn't learnt her lesson; she will still run in front of my chair. But I take more care when the puppies are running around. At least Angel has the sense to get out the way.

Chapter 4

'You'll Never Walk Again'

Why operations are risky when you have the body of an old person

People who know me think I am happy all the time, but that's just not true. I do try my best to stay positive but sometimes it's just not possible. Take, for example, the time I needed a hip-replacement operation. I guess some of you may be already be wondering why I am now in a wheelchair when I used to walk about all the time, right?

If you have read my other book *Old Before My Time* you may remember that just as I hit my teens, I started having problems with my hips. That's the trouble with having the bones of a 136-year-old – you get old people's problems! I never thought that when I tripped over a bench in the school gym and hurt my leg, I would never walk properly ever again. The fall made my left hip 'pop' out of its socket. The school called an ambulance to take me to hospital, which was really annoying because all the other kids started spreading rumours that I had died. I remember the pain was just horrible. I was crying so much, but the only thing the ambulance men could give me to ease the pain was gas and air. At first I refused because I was too scared. I had seen things on TV where people breathe in gas and go really loopy and I didn't want that to happen. But the pain got so bad that I just didn't know what to do with myself. Mum said, 'Why don't you try the gas and air? I had some when you were born and it didn't make me mad.' Normally I would have thought of something sarcastic to say, but I was in too much pain. I just nodded and Mum handed me a rubber mask. I held it to my face and breathed in. It went all quiet in the room, then after a couple of seconds I started giggling and the pain didn't seem so bad.

19

At the hospital the doctor took me into a side ward and told me he was going to squirt a couple of drops of morphine up my nose to ease the pain while they decided what they were going to do with me. They were worried that my bones would be so weak they might break them and they weren't sure how much anaesthetic to give me, which was a bit worrying. I was thirteen but my body was smaller than an average seven-year-old. While we waited Mum and Louis stayed with me. I felt really out of it, but could still feel the pain.

'It really hurts, Mum, can't they give me something stronger,' I asked. Mum told me there wasn't anything stronger than morphine, which was not good. Every time I cried, Louis held my hand and rubbed my head. It was so cute it made me cry harder. It must have been scary for him and it made me feel bad as I didn't want my brother to be worried.

Eventually the doctor came to give me the anaesthetic injection before the operation he said:

'Count down from ten and soon you'll be asleep.'

I counted right down to one and I was still awake. I was frightened that the anaesthetic wasn't going to work.

'Please make sure I wake up,' I said to Mum as they wheeled me into theatre. 'If I don't wake up, Maddie's going to come and get me.'

I often think about my friend when I'm scared or worried.

'Maddie's not ready for you yet, you're coming back to Mummy. Promise me you'll come back to Mummy.'

The last thing I saw as they wheeled me out to theatre was Mum crying and holding on to the door. It's not a nice feeling to know that your family are upset or worried about you. I didn't want to make them sad. It scared me.

I woke up, choking. There was a tube in my mouth and I couldn't breathe. I must have gone back to sleep because the next thing I was awake and the tube had gone but my throat was really sore. I saw Mum and was happy.

'Can I have an iPad?' were my first words.

I may have been half out of it but I hadn't forgotten that she promised to get me one when I was crying in pain.

Unfortunately that wasn't the end of it. It kept happening. One time I was just walking up the stairs to my dad's flat and they 'popped out'. My hips dislocated so often that Mum and the doctors used to joke that I had my own VIP room at the Conquest Hospital's A&E department. It got to the point where I couldn't walk anywhere without wearing a metal brace to hold my bones in place. I hated that stupid brace. It was purple and ugly. 'Here comes Robo-Chick,' Mum would say, to make me feel better, but it only made me feel worse. The only good thing about wearing the brace was that I didn't have to go to school for a year. I think Mum was worried that I might fall and hurt myself again, so she made arrangements with the school for me to have lessons over the internet.

'I don't feel well today,' I would say when I woke up with aching legs.

So Mum would let me sit on the sofa all day, watching *Come Dine With Me* on TV, instead of doing lessons. For the first couple of weeks while I was off school, my best friend Erin came to visit and we would watch TV together. Erin and I had been friends since we were nearly four years old. We met on our first day at Bexhill Primary School and we'd been friends ever since. Erin would come round and tell me all the school gossip, so I didn't feel like I was missing out. But as the weeks dragged into months, my friend stopped visiting.

Mum was convinced that there was an operation I could have to give me new hips so that I could walk properly again. For months we went back and fore to see Dr Hinves, my orthopaedic surgeon at the Conquest Hospital in Hastings. He had a plastic model of a hip bone on his desk, which he used to explain my problem.

'Normally there is a cup-shaped socket in the hip and there is a ball shape on the top of your leg bone,' he said, pointing to the skeleton model. 'These fit together and are held in place with muscles and ligaments. But in your case those muscles and ligaments are so loose they can't hold the bones in place. We could operate but there's no guarantee it wouldn't pop back out.'

Dr Hinves referred me to see one of the top children's orthopaedic specialists at the Evalina Children's Hospital in London. They examined my hips, asked lots of questions and took X-rays of my old bones. During one of these consultations I was asked to lie down on the table, while a doctor I hadn't seen before felt my hips. I lay there while he wiggled my legs around. Suddenly I cried out, 'Ow, that really hurt.' My leg had popped out of the socket and the pain was horrible. The doctor was really, really sorry and popped my bone back in the socket, which hurt even more.

'I thought doctors were supposed to make you better, not hurt you,' Mum whispered to me as we left the room.

'Don't ever let them do that to me again,' I said.

At one of the many hospital appointments, we were shown X-rays of my hips. Now I'm no doctor but even I could tell that my hip bones were rubbish.

'As you can see, your hips are set at an angle and the sockets are shallow, which is common for Progeria children,' the doctor explained. 'As a result they can't hold the bone in place, which is the reason your hips keep popping out. There is an operation we can do but it would mean cutting the top of your femur or thigh bone to realign it,' he said 'We would have to operate on one leg at a time. Each operation will take six hours.'

Me and Mum sat there taking it all in. I was excited to think that I would be able to walk again without my brace, but I didn't like the idea of being in an operation for six hours. I could tell by the look on her face, that Mum was worried too.

'What are the risks?' Mum asked.

'For someone like Hayley there is a greater risk than a normal person. Getting the dose of anaesthetic correct will be difficult as she is almost an adult but with the body of a child half her age. There is also the possibility that her skin is so thin that the wound will not heal properly and cause infection. For someone of Hayley's body size, that could be a problem.'

My skin has always been thin. That was one of the things that Mum noticed when I was baby before doctors told her I had Hutchinson-Gilford progeria. She used to say that my belly looked like it was covered in cling film. Kids with progeria don't have the same stretchiness in their skin as normal people.

'Is there a chance she won't wake up after the operation?' Mum asked.

'The risk of dying is very low for a healthy person or child: it would be less than 1 in 100,000. Hayley's heart is strong, she is healthy, her blood pressure is normal, but with all surgery there is

Queen of the fairies at the Progeria Reunion
in Ashford, Kent (2010)

Photo by Legend Photography

I think Louis is trying to tell me something (2011)

The 'not so big sister' with Ruby and Louis (2011)

My pet Chihuahua, Boo, hitching a lift (2013)

Angel trying to steal my toys (2012)

One of Boo's puppies (2013)

Who's taking whom for a walk?
Me, Angel and Boo out walking
on the coastal path above
Eastbourne (2012)

Nanna with Mollie and Dollie

My last day at
Bexhill High
School
(May 2014)

My first day at Sidley
Primary School, left,
(2001) and, above, my
first day at Bexhill High
School (2009)

Ever get the feeling you're being watched?

Checking Twitter in the sun at the Progeria Reunion in Montegrotto Terme near Venice, Italy (2012)

Family day out with Louis and Ruby at classic car show in Bexhill (2012)

Me and my 'little' sister Ruby on my sixteenth birthday
(December 2013)

Me, Mum, Ruby and Louis on the merry-go-round on a day out
at Thorpe Park (2009)

Getting stuck into baking (2013)

A day out at the Bentley Wildfowl Park in Sussex (2013)

Inside the motor museum at the Bentley Wildfowl Park (2013)

Me and my friend Harry
Crowther (2013)

Mum inspecting my Prom
dress disaster (2014)

The launch day of my first book *Old Before My Time* and a present from my publisher (2011)

On the way to the Prom with Luke and my posh ride (2014)

My best friend Courtney and me at the Prom (2014)

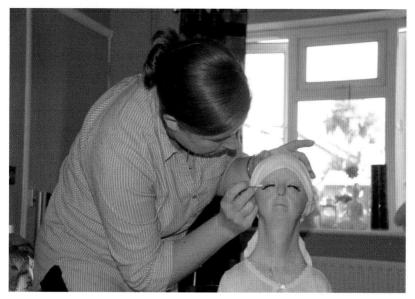

Mum's friend Amie helps me get made up for Prom Night
(2014)

My Prom date: brother Luke (2014)

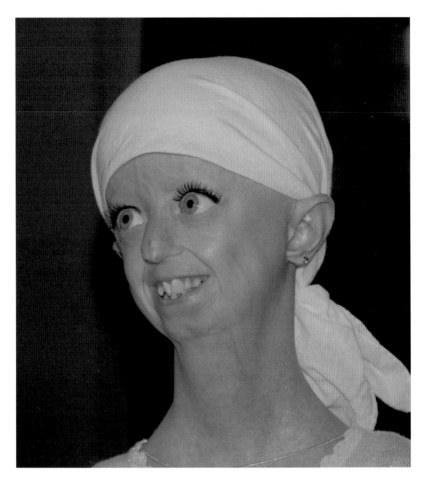

My Prom (2014)

always a risk. Of course I can arrange a consultation with the anaesthetist if you would like to ask more questions.'

'And supposing we decide to go through with the operation, what are her chances of walking again?' Mum asked.

'Thirty per cent,' was the reply.

Maths isn't my strongest subject, but even I could work out that a less than a one-in-three chance was not good. I would be knocked out for twelve hours for the operations and that was if nothing went wrong. Would I wake up? What if I went through all of that and still couldn't walk? I thought about how scared I had been and how heartbroken Mum was when I had gone into the operating theatre after the first dislocation and that was only for twenty minutes. She had been worried that I would not wake up then.

All the way home I thought about what the doctor had said. Back at the house I sat down with Mum and Dad and we talked about what to do.

'Why can't they just put superglue on the ball and stick it back again?' Louis asked.

'If only it was that easy,' said Mum.

We weighed up the things that could go wrong against the things that could go right. Infections, anaesthetic, complications, it all sounded a bit too scary. From what I could see there were more negatives than positives.

'They wouldn't operate on a hundred-year-old as their bodies aren't strong enough,' Mum said. 'If only the odds of you being to walk again were fifty-fifty it would be better.'

'I don't want to do it,' I said finally.

Nearly all my life I've had hospital tests for the drug trials in Boston and regular check-ups with my heart doctor, but the thought of having such a big operation had scared me. Once I had made up my mind, I was sad but relieved. I think Mum was more disappointed. She had set her heart on me walking like a normal teenager.

Chapter 5

'Now I Have an Excuse to Be Extra Lazy'

What it's really like to lose the use of your legs

It's funny because I always imagined my first driving experience would be behind the wheel of a bright pink VW Beetle or a flaming red Mini – not some hospital-issue wheelchair. I suppose I shouldn't moan, I'm lucky that I can move myself around when I want to. It's just that when you have always been able to run around, ride a bike and stuff, being told you will never walk again is really, really depressing.

At first the hospital gave me a walking frame on wheels that fitted around my back, which I could hold on to walk around the house. Mum would make me use it to walk to the toilet, but my arms were so weak I found it hard to hold on to it. It took me so long to shuffle down the hallway that my legs would really ache by the time I got there, so I needed to sit down!

'If you don't use your muscles, they'll just waste away, then you won't be able to do anything for yourself,' Mum warned.

'Would you rather I fell and dislocated my hip again? I snapped back.

I hated being so useless. I couldn't even go to my bedroom because I couldn't climb the stairs. Every morning was the same: Mum would have to physically get me out of bed, carry me down the stairs and sit me on the sofa in front of the TV. She would even have to carry me into the shower. I felt like there was nothing to look forward to. For someone who is always being told 'you're so happy' I was really miserable.

Mum arranged some physiotherapy sessions for me at Conquest Hospital. She would drop me off for my session and the therapist would get me to walk across the room, holding on to two poles like gymnast. Once I managed to walk five lengths of the room, but my arms and legs ached so much afterwards that I gave up. I think Mum was pushing me to walk because she didn't want to be running around after me forever. But that was a fact of life. I had to accept I would never walk again. I had to suck it up and get on with life.

Around the same time some of my Progeria friends were also facing similar problems. Michiel, who is a year younger than me and lives in Belgium, had always loved playing soccer, but he had to stop playing for his team because he kept dislocating his shoulder and was afraid of hurting himself. His parents also had to get a special battery for his bike so that he could keep up with his friends because his joints were hurting when he pedalled. Another friend had a special walker made …

Accepting I would never walk again was one thing, but when the time came to be measured up for my own wheelchair I cried and cried.

'I really don't want to do it, Mum,' I sobbed. It was such a big change. I'd run around and walked all my life. The thought of being stuck in a wheelchair for the rest of my life was no fun. It was really horrible and depressing. I didn't want to be treated differently. I hated the thought of going back to school and all the kids asking, 'What's wrong with you? Why are you in that? Can you walk?' Plus I was helping Mum's friend organise a charity Masquerade Ball to raise money for our Progeria Reunion (more of this later). I had already bought my red satin dress and I really wanted to walk in and make a grand entrance. Arriving in a wheelchair with Mum or Dad pushing me wasn't what I had in mind. I didn't want people looking at me. I dreaded going back to school. It had been almost a year since I had last walked into my class.

But I didn't have much choice in the matter and the hospital provided me with an adult-sized chair that was way too big. There was no way I could push myself around; I could hardly reach the rims of the wheels. I had to depend on my family and friends to take me everywhere.

Back at school people started asking all the questions I had been afraid of. Why are you in the wheelchair? What happened? Have you got to stay in that forever?

'I don't want to talk about it, just leave me alone,' I told them.

I so hated it. Looking back I can see that they were only trying to be nice, but at the time it was such a big change and I was just getting used to it and didn't want to answer their questions.

Next Mum suggested we should go and try out a special disabled bath seat.

'There's a shop in Eastbourne that sells mobility aids,' she said. 'We can get a seat that fits on the bath; it will be easier than having me carry you into the shower.'

'No way,' I said and started crying. Mum insisted it would be better. So off to Eastbourne we went. When she pulled up outside the shop, I was horrified. The window was full of Zimmer frames, walking sticks and chairs for old people.

'I don't want one. I hate them.' They were made for grown-ups and were too big.

Mum: 'But you have to have a bath seat.'

Me: 'Why!

Mum: 'Because I can't carry on lifting you in and out of the shower. One day we'll both slip and have an accident.'

Me: 'Why can't we just have a shower at Auntie Janie's house? I like it when you and me have a shower at Auntie Janie's and she lifts me out and dries me with a big fluffy towel.'

Mum: 'You have to have a shower more than once a fortnight, you stinking mare.'

Once she coaxed me inside the shop Mum told me to lift myself on to the seat.

'I can't do it,' I said.

'Yes, you can,' said Mum.

'No I can't,' I was getting really annoyed. It was like she thought I could still do these things and I couldn't and that made it worse.

After I had a bath seat, Mum decided that I needed an electric wheelchair. She thought that I would be more independent if I could drive myself around as my arms were not strong enough to move my 'pushy wheelchair'. But when she looked into it, she discovered they cost anything from £4,000 to £25,000, which seemed like a lot of money. I thought I could get a really nice car instead. I knew we couldn't afford that kind of money, so I didn't worry too much until one day Mum came home and asked me what colour wheelchair I wanted.

'I don't care,' I cried. 'I told you I didn't want an electric wheelchair.'

But it turned out that our local Cooden Beach Golf Club held something called the Peter Alliss Masters Powered Wheelchair Crusade charity golf tournament every year to raise money to buy electric wheelchairs for people, and they wanted to buy one for me.

Mum had to drag me down to the presentation evening at the club. I really didn't want to go. There were six other kids, all with different problems and we all had to line up and have our photos taken. I really didn't feel in the mood to smile for the cameras. My grandparents, Nanna and Pops, were there too and Pops had to persuade me to try it out. I wasn't bothered at all.

'Just give it a try,' Pops said, lifting me into the new chair.

There was a joystick thing on the right arm. Pops moved it forward, and the chair whizzed ahead.

'This could be fun' I thought.

It was a bit like how I imagined it would be learning to drive. When I pushed it the gear stick backwards, the chair reversed. I moved it to the right and the chair started to turn. Before I knew it I was driving.

Back home, I had a few accidents as I learnt to drive the thing. I scraped the paint off the door frames and tore wallpaper off the walls as I tried to drive myself in and out of the living room. After a while I got used to it and could manage to get down the hallway and into the kitchen. But once I got to the kitchen I realised that I couldn't actually reach the cupboards or the work top because my arms were too short.

'What you need is a chair that can move up and down,' said Mum.

It was all part of her plan to get me doing more for myself. She went online and found out about a charity called Whizz Kidz, which buys wheelchairs and mobility aids for people like me. They sent a woman around to see me and measure up what I needed. After a couple of months they presented me with a bigger Spectra wheelchair. It was massive and had a chair seat which could raise me up and forward. It took some getting used to. Once I raised it too quickly and squashed my legs under the kitchen work top.

Another time I crashed into the kitchen cupboards as the floor was wet and I was going too fast. There is just one small problem; I still can't reach the wall cupboards where we keep our dishes, so Mum has to leave stuff out for me to make my own breakfast.

Another part of Mum's mission to make me more independent was getting the council, who own our house, to install an electric lift so that I can get up on my own in the morning. Have I told you that I hate getting up in the mornings? The best thing about the lift was that I got to swap to Louis's bigger bedroom. The worst thing was that we had to lose half of our dining room. The lift looks like a TARDIS or something. It's a big square metal box in the corner of the room, with a door that swings open and closes behind me. Our neighbour who lives across the road says she can hear when I'm getting up, because it makes such a loud clunking noise. But at least I don't have to wait for Mum to carry me up and downstairs any more.

Until you're actually in a wheelchair you don't realise how hard it is to get around or how inconsiderate some people can be. For example a lot of the shops in Bexhill have steps to get into them, so it's difficult for me to go shopping on my own. Some of the newer shopping centres in Eastbourne are easier to get around as they are flat and have loads of room inside. Even getting around the house can be a problem, especially if Ruby or Louis leave things hanging around on the floor and I can't drive over them.

We had to swap our ordinary Ford Focus for a super big, seven-seat estate car so that we have enough room for my chair. Our new car is fitted with an electric hoist which makes it easier for Mum to get my chair in and out. She used to have two telescopic metal ramps that she kept in the boot and had to pull out to drive my wheelchair into the back. She was always getting into a state when she was on her own because my chair is so heavy. It weights 120kg, which is almost ten times as heavy as I am. Sometimes she would ask Dad to help which made it a bit easier.

Whenever we go out shopping, Mum always parks where there's loads of space around, so that she can get my wheelchair in and out of the boot. But she gets really mad whenever someone parks right behind her and doesn't leave her enough room. Then she has to drive out in the middle of the road and load me and the chair into the car, which can be really scary, especially when there's a queue of traffic waiting to get past. 'They'll just have to wait,' she says when some impatient drivers beep their horn at her. See what I mean about inconsiderate?

The best thing about being in a wheelchair is I that now have an excuse to be extra lazy. If I'm tired I will play on it by asking people to run around and do things for me. I think Mum is having more difficulty coming to terms with the fact I will never walk again than I am. She says things like, 'I really wish you could walk again. I miss it when you used to run up behind me in the kitchen when I wasn't expecting it.' She's always looking at old photos of me before I had my wheelchair. Sometimes she even dreams of me walking. Isn't that sad?

Chapter 6

'I'm Happy With My One Friend'

My thoughts on going out and socialising

I am such an awkward person, it's really bad. I'd like to make friends but my awkwardness stops me. Courtney is my only really close friend. We have known each other since primary school. I don't even remember how we met but we have been friends since Year Five. I like Courtney for lots of reasons but I'm not very good at explaining them. I think it's because we are so similar that we just clicked. Obviously we don't look similar. Courtney has long brown hair and brown eyes. In the summer her hair goes lighter and she gets freckles on her face. I tease her that she is secretly blonde.

We understand each other. Courtney says she doesn't notice that I am different from anyone else; to her I'm just another friend. Courtney has an older brother and sister and a younger brother and sister who are twins. The twins look so cute with their big smiles and dimples, but they are nearly the same age as Ruby so I get it when Courtney says they're evil. I know what it's like to live with horrible younger siblings. It gets me annoyed when people think Ruby is really nice because she's not. And Courtney goes through the same with her sister.

'The twins are really nice to me when they want something,' Courtney says.

Her younger brother is really cheeky. Honestly I don't know where these younger brothers and sisters get their attitudes from.

Courtney is a really loyal friend. When we were still at school we would see each other every day. And even if she was doing things with her other friends she would always text me. We mostly stay in the house or walk to the shops as we don't have a lot of money to go out all the time. When we are not together I will send a picture of my favourite band or send her a link and say, 'Please buy this song.' Then Courtney will text back 'No, I can't afford it.' So I'll say, 'Please, just listen to it.' And she'll say, 'I don't want to know. I don't want to start liking them.'

Courtney says she can't afford to like loads of bands as it costs too much money to buy all their CDs and posters and concert tickets. So she just sticks to her one favourite band Lawson. I like Lawson but I like loads of other bands, too, so I'll text her 'Please just look at this picture' and send a photo message of a really cute band member from The Wanted, The Vamps or 5 Seconds of Summer (5SOS) , who are currently my favourite bands. 'Look at his face, please. ' And Courtney will reply, 'Go away. End of conversation.'

All through primary school my best friend was Erin, we always said that when we left school we would move to New York or Hawaii and open a beauty salon together. But when I stopped going to school, we lost touch. After being away from school for so long, when I went back Erin had different lessons and different friends, so we just stop talking. She texted me a long time afterwards to say she was sorry she hadn't kept in touch.

'You left me when I really needed you the most,' I told her.

I felt a bit let down. We had been friends for so long but we'd grown apart, we liked different things. She is into boys and going out, and I'm into boy bands and staying in, so that's all there is to it. We don't hate each other or anything like that.

I'm quite happy just having the one friend; although I do have a best friend on Twitter called Shannon (I'll explain more about Shannon later). Mum is always trying to get me to go out and make friends. She thought it would be a good idea to sign me up for a buddy scheme run by our local hospice, Demelza James House. I haven't been the hospice for years, not since I was about seven or eight. When I was little we used to go there as a family for weekends, it was like having a holiday. They had a Jacuzzi there – or 'kajuzzi' as I used to call it – and a big soft play room where I could run and jump around without hurting myself. It was at the hospice I first saw children in wheelchairs. They used to shout a lot and scared me until a nurse explained that they had learning difficulties and couldn't help it.

Anyway this woman with dreadlocks and peace signs hanging from her ears came to our house to talk to me and Mum about the Demelza James House buddy scheme.

'We have a mini-bus that's specially adapted for wheelchairs. We have a group of young people who are Hayley's age and we take them out on trips. Sometimes we'll go bowling or to the cinema,' she said.

She was so bubbly; I thought she was going to burst. Mum was asking lots of questions about the other children and the facilities. I could tell by the look on her face that she was excited, so I stayed quiet.

'Sounds good, doesn't it?' she said after the woman had left.

'If I want to go out, I will go out with Courtney, I don't want to go out with a group of people I don't even know. And anyway I'm not disabled,' I said. That was the last I heard of that stupid idea.

It's not that I can't go out, I just don't want to. There's nothing to do in Bexhill apart from going to the cinema, which is so expensive. I could go to the park all day but that gets boring. In the winter it is freezing, so why would I want to go out when I can stay at home and be warm. In the summer Courtney and I like to go shopping to Eastbourne. We get the train from Bexhill, which only takes about thirty minutes. The people working at the station know me so they help me to get my wheelchair on the train with ramps. Then they help me get off the other end. I like Eastbourne: it's got much better shops than Bexhill. They've got a Primark, where they have lots of cool clothes, Claire's, where I get cute clips and accessories for my bandana, and my favourite of all, HMV, where I always come away with a new poster or something.

When we go shopping I have to ask Mum to give me money from my bank account, that's where she saves all the money I have been paid from magazine appearances, TV documentaries and royalties from my last book *Old Before My Time*.

I'll say, 'Can I have some money to go shopping?'

She'll say, 'How much do you want?'

I say, '£20' expecting her to knock it down to £10.

And she says, 'Why don't you take £50?'

And I say 'No, £20 is enough.'

Mum says I need to learn the value of money but she doesn't

really mind if I spend my money on going to concerts all the time. I'm really lucky because most kids my age have to fight with their parents to get pocket money.

Chapter 7

'I Wouldn't Say I Hated School, But I'm Glad I Don't Have to Go Back'

Reflections on my high school years

May 23 2014: One of the happiest days of my life: the last day at Bexhill High School. It was funny to watch all the people crying and hugging each other as if it was the end of the world and they would never see each other ever again. I didn't cry, I was just happy to go home.

That day Mum posted two photos of me on Facebook and asked, 'Where has 16 years gone?' The first photo was taken on my first day at Bexhill Primary School, when I was four. I'm standing in front of the sofa in our living room, wearing a tiny blue and white checked pinafore, navy cardigan and navy bandana, holding a Powerpuff Girls lunchbox. The box is almost as big as me and I'm grinning. In the other photo I am sitting in my wheelchair on the path leading up to Bexhill High. I'm wearing my black jogging pants and black hoodie, with the hood up. Believe it or not I'm still smiling. But that's more to do with the fact that I will never, ever have to sit through another maths or English lesson again.

Unlike most kids my age, I wouldn't say I hated school. I actually like learning new stuff; I just don't like waking up in the mornings. I started Bexhill High when I was eleven and could still walk around. In those days I had lots of friends who used to look out for me in the playground and make sure I didn't get knocked over by the older boys and their footballs. I also had a special friend, Mrs Gilbert. Mrs G, as I've always called her, wasn't a teacher but she looked after me every day in high school. Her official title was a teaching assistant, but she used to say she was more like my 'slave'. When we first met she had never heard of

Progeria or seen any of my documentaries on TV, but she googled me. 'I wanted to see what I was getting myself into,' she once told me. We hit it off straight away, I liked her sarcasm.

The more I got to know Mrs G, the more I realised how much we had in common. We had the same sense of humour, we were both sarcastic. When we teased each other, it was like our way of showing affection. If we like you, we tease you. We spent most of our time together making fun of each other. Deep down we were like best friends, although neither of us would admit it.

In the first years, when I could still walk around, Mrs G used to look out for me during the break times and make sure that I didn't get knocked over in the mad rush to get out of classes and stuff. But when I couldn't walk, she would meet me at the school entrance every morning and stay with me all through lessons until Mum or Dad came to pick me up at home time.

As schools go, Bexhill High wasn't too bad. It was a good place to for me to fit in. It wasn't like a regular school; it's what they call an academy school. The building was brand new and looked more like a leisure centre or something with wide corridors and lifts, so it was easy to get around in my electric chair. People used to dive out of the way when they saw me coming. Once I ran over someone's foot, I wasn't sure who it was as there were so many people around. I just felt a bump. I said, 'So sorry. Are you OK?' They didn't shout at me, so I think they were OK.

At Bexhill High the classes were really big, with up to ninety kids at a time, all sitting in groups of five or six at round white plastic tables on blue and yellow plastic chairs. It sounds a bit crazy, but mostly it seemed to work. I would sit in the front of the classroom with Mrs G, because it was easier to get my wheelchair in and out and I could hear the teacher better. I knew my space and everyone was happy with that.

When I was younger I had a dream that I would open a beauty salon. So when, at the start of year ten, I had to make my career choices, I chose hair and beauty. The school arranged for me to have a special chair that rose up and down and a tiny hairdryer so that I could learn hairdressing. But after a couple of weeks I realised that it wasn't what I wanted to do, so Mum asked the school if I could change my subjects. Usually students aren't allowed to swap and have to choose four subjects as well as maths,

English and science, but I only had to pick two. I guess that's one of the perks of having progeria, you don't have to follow the same rules as everyone else. So I chose food technology and art. They were both my favourite subjects. I enjoyed cooking and had a special cooker and work top in the food technology room. It had a handle that could be made lower than everyone else so I could reach. I especially loved the art room, it had so much natural light, and I would sit in front of the massive windows in the summer and looking out on the trees and the birds in the sky. Mrs G was a good artist. Sometimes we'd be sitting in class and I would be drawing something that looked rubbish and I'd look over at Mrs G and she had drawn something amazing. I wished I could swap my work for hers; I would have so much better marks. But Mrs G told me that wasn't allowed.

Every day in school there would be some new argument. Mrs G and I didn't get involved. We just sat together in our space and placed bets on who was going to win and who was going to get beaten up first. One day in the middle of an English lesson, when we were reading the Sherlock Holmes book *The Hound of the Baskervilles*, two boys decided to hide in the book cupboard. They emptied out the books, took out all the shelves and climbed inside. Then another guy got a computer lead and tied the handles together so they couldn't get out. They were just left sitting in the cupboard and everyone was acting as if nothing had happened. When the teacher untied them and told them to get out, they just walked back to their seats. The teacher wasn't amused, even though it was quite funny. Another time there was a massive fight between a group of girls who were arguing over some pointless TV programme. I said nothing.

'You're very wise not to get involved,' Mrs G said.

There were plenty of things about school that annoyed me, like maths, for example. I hated maths anyway and when I started doing my GCSEs, they put me in a lower group. It was so boring, but then Mum had a word with the teachers and they moved me up to a C grade set, which was a bit better. The thing that really annoyed me about maths was the actual maths room, which probably sounds weird. But on the wall there was a row of paper cut-out numbers counting down from ten to minus ten. I know you're thinking, so what? And that would have been OK, but all the numbers were the same size, except for the tens at either end.

'That's just wrong. The numbers should all be the same size,' I kept telling Mrs G.

It annoyed me so much that sometimes I found it hard to sit in the classroom and focus. Mrs G said we should 'do a Banksy' in the middle of the night and change the numbers to the right size. Another thing that really bugged me around school was the way some people would leave electricity sockets switched on when there was nothing plugged into them. That's just dangerous. I couldn't concentrate on my work until Mrs G switched them off for me.

During the break and lunch times, while most of the other kids would head down to the dining area, I would stay in the classroom with Mrs G. The food area was in the middle of the school and was really bright with shiny metal tables and chairs, food stands at both ends and ping-pong tables in the centre. The lights there were so bright that they hurt my eyes, so I used to spend most of my breaks in the classroom. I'm such a loner.

In school there were loads of rules on what you could and couldn't wear. No jeans, no jeggings, no studs, no zips, no sequins, no buttons or piping on your trousers, no labels on either your trousers or your shoes. Shoes had to be black with heels less than 3cm. Skirts had to be less than 4cm above the knee and no more than 7cm below. Facial or body piercings, tattoos, nail varnish and false nails weren't allowed. You couldn't wear hoodies, hats or caps and couldn't have dyed hair or 'extreme' hairstyles, whatever that meant. At the start of the term, the whole school would have to stand in line while the teachers checked for nail varnish and made sure we were all wearing proper shoes. Some kids who were wearing black Vans shoes were told to take them off or cover the logo with black sticky tape. Girls who had pockets on their trousers were told to take them off. I mean, how stupid is that? If you take a patch pocket off your trousers everyone will see your underwear.

'You get away with pretty much anything,' Courtney used to say to me. Sometimes I used to tease Courtney because we'd be sitting together in class and a teacher would walk past and tell her to take off the vest top she was wearing *under* her school polo shirt. Yet I would be sitting there wearing a bright pink hoodie and they wouldn't say anything to me. I guess that's another of the perks of having progeria.

Mum says I get away with more than most students. 'We only live once, so why shouldn't you get special treatment,' is her attitude, so she used to let me wear nail polish and necklaces to school. Once I wore a purple bandana to school. None of the teachers said anything to me, but I knew it didn't look good. It had started out white but Mum washed it with Ruby's purple jeans and it changed colour. Over the years I was pulled up a couple of times about the uniform rules. Once I was ordered to cover up the pink Nike logos on my trainers and I was told off for wearing nail polish. But that wasn't my fault. I like having painted nails but I don't like rubbing anything on my nails as it makes me cringe. It's one of those things, just like my Mum says she can't touch flour and some people can't stand the sound of chalk scratching on blackboards. So I can't physically use nail varnish remover to wipe it off. I had to ask someone else to do it for me, which always seemed like a good excuse to me, even if the teachers didn't think so.

Over the years Mrs G got to know me so well, she could tell if I needed something without me ever having to ask her. It would have been so annoying if I had to ask for every time I needed her to pass me a pen or book, but Mrs G would just get on and do it. She could tell just by looking at my face when I got lost in class, which mostly happened in maths, my least favourite subject. The teacher would be saying 'XY equals blah blah blah' and Mrs G would look at me and say, 'It's okay, I'll tell you later.' So I just sat there, nodding. It was like having two brains and an extra pair of ears.

I can't imagine what school would have been like if my teaching assistant was grumpy or didn't get my sarcastic sense of humour. I think Mrs G is one of the reasons I enjoyed my time at Bexhill High. She said I've shown her loads of new things, mostly silly photos on my phone. I've shown her a ferret in a hoodie, a kitten in a bowl, a tomato shaped like a duck and some bee's knees. She now knows more about my favourite bands The Wanted, The Vamps, Green Day and 5SOS than she'll ever need to know. She knows which member of The Wanted likes lizards and who drinks Guinness. I also shared with her all the things I learnt from watching weird science programmes and documentaries on TV with my dad.

For example:

Me: 'If you had to choose between swimming in a lake of acid or alkaline, what would you do?'

Mrs G: 'Well, I would prefer not to swim in either.'

Me: 'I would choose acid because it would only burn a couple of layers of skin, but the alkali carries on burning.'

Mrs G: 'I hope I never have to find out.'

In return Mrs G taught me patience and how to be annoyed with someone without showing it, which I imagine will be very useful in the future.

When I got home on the last day of school, I started unpacking my bag and noticed an envelope with my name written on it in Mrs G's neat handwriting. She must have slipped it in my bag when I wasn't looking, I thought. I opened it and saw that Mrs G had used her amazing art skills to draw a picture of a cartoon turtle (my favourite animal of the moment) wearing big blue glasses. It said 'Have a Turtley Cool Time!' I opened it up and read the message.

'I'm discombobulated,' she wrote. (See, she knew me so well that she knew my favourite word.) It continued, 'We started at Bexhill High within a couple of weeks of each other and we've worked together ever since. You know that you will honestly be missed so much. Your wit, your enthusiasm and your interest, you are such a pleasure to be around ... and of course your infectious laugh. The way you have worked this year is truly amazing! You have worked so hard and you have achieved so much – congratulations! Wishing you all the very best for your college course and future – you'll do brilliantly. Have fun, stay safe and enjoy life (and stay in touch).

Love and best wishes

Mrs G'

I wiped my wet face with my sleeve. I was glad she hadn't given me the card in person, as I knew I would cry. I wondered if Mrs G had been just as sad when she had opened the card I had given her and read what I had written. I told her, 'Thank you for not just being my TA, but my best friend. I hope you do something with your drawing skills – they are too good to waste.'

I do miss Mrs G. She knew me so well; I hope we will stay in touch. She says that now I can call her by her real name, Tracey, but she will always be Mrs G to me – even when I'm old, like thirty.

Chapter 8

'Who Says I Can't Wear Trainers to a Prom?'

My thoughts on dressing up and partying

'What do you mean, you're not going? Courtney said to me one day during the school lunch break. 'You've got to go to the Prom.'

'It's just not my thing,' I said, and hoped that would be the end of the matter.

The Prom was being held at the Powder Mills Hotel in Bexhill on 3rd July 2014. It was five months away, so I had plenty of time to come up with an excuse. But Courtney kept on.

'Please, you've got to go. It's the biggest night of the school year. It will be the last time our year will all be together. Why not?'

'For one thing I don't own a dress and I'm not really into the girl thing of dressing up and wearing loads of make-up.'

When I was younger, like seven or eight, I used to love getting made up. Mum would help me put on make-up and I would pretend to be Princess Hayley. But as I got older I was more aware of how I look different from other girls. The thought of spending money on a ticket, then having to buy a dress that I was never ever going to wear again, would mean wasting loads of money. Money that I could spend on something I would actually enjoy like concert tickets or posters of boy bands.

'All right,' I finally gave in. 'I will go – but only if Nathan Sykes takes me.'

At the time Nathan was my favourite member of my favourite-ever band The Wanted. He follows me on Twitter, so I sent him a DM and asked him if he would be my partner for the prom.

'When is it?' he tweeted back.

'July 3' I messaged.

A couple of weeks later I went to see the band in concert at

Brighton and got to meet them. When I saw Nathan backstage he promised he would take me if he could. The closer it got to the Prom, I decided that even if Nathan didn't take me I would still go. When I told Mrs G that I was going, she said she would like to go but she was banned. Her daughter was in the same year and didn't want her there. I could see her point. I wouldn't want my mum to go either. It would be too embarrassing to see your mum getting drunk and dancing at your prom.

Once I bought my ticket, I had to find something to wear. I looked on the internet and saw a great dress on eBay. It was only £50 and looked really nice. Mum said, 'You should go to a shop and buy one, so you can see what you're getting.'

'But it's really nice and they'll make it to fit me in any colour I want,' I said.

So Mum gave in and I placed my order. In my head I had an idea of a beautiful off-the shoulder, ruched silk bodice with lots of sparkles and the same flowing material. When the parcel arrived from China I was so excited. I ripped open the bubble wrap. It was lovely. The top half was lilac with diagonal pleats across the front and a white sequinned section, stitched into a massive bow at the waist. But when I pulled it out of its packaging, my heart sank. The bottom half was so cheap. It was made of pink-and-white triangles of that awful scratchy nylon-netting material sewn on to a white satin skirt. You could see all the stitches where the nasty lace was sewn on. I wanted to cry. I looked at Mum and Dad, they were trying not to laugh and that made me even more upset.

'I told you not to buy it off the internet,' Mum said, in a kind of 'I told you so' way.

'Maybe Nanna can fix it,' I said.

My Nanna is really clever. She used to work as a school cook and bakes lovely cookies and gingerbread. When I was little I used to sleep over with Nanna and Pops every weekend and sometimes she would take me out shopping. I remember being so excited once when Nanna bought me this bright pink tutu dress, which was way too big, but I wanted it so much she bought it for me anyway. Whenever I wore it Nanna used to say I looked like a meringue on a lollipop stick. I thought if anyone could save my prom dress, Nanna could. So we showed the dress to Nanna.

'Can you do anything with this?' Mum asked Nanna.

'Yeah. Throw it in the bin,' she laughed. I was so upset, I had wasted £50.

At school, all the talk was about the prom. Courtney had bought her outfit and she was going to look amazing. So Mum took me out shopping to Eastbourne to find a replacement for my dress disaster. We went into a couple of shops and all we could find were full-length, flowing dresses. The more we looked, the more depressed I became.

'Mum, why are we even looking? None of these will fit me,' I said.

They were all made to fit your average-sized teenager, not a seven-year-old.

Then I turned around and there it was. Aqua blue, the same colour as my eyes, and made from a light, floaty material. It was perfect. It had a sequinned waistband and the pleated bodice was held up by the thinnest, spaghetti straps. I know this sounds stupid, but I got butterflies in my stomach just looking at it. And, even better, they had it in a size 4. I was so excited. Mum held the dress in front of me. It was just the right length, the skirt reached below my knees. The top was a bit big but Mum said, 'It's got elastic at the back, so I can sew you into it.' At £65, it was a bargain.

'Now all I need is a cardigan and shoes to go with it,' I said. We found a silver and white cardigan that matched rather nicely and went looking for shoes. Most of the other girls would be wearing high heels, but none of the shoes I tried on looked right. I didn't want to wear tights, and ankle socks looked too childish.

'Why don't you wear your Converse,' Mum unhelpfully suggested.

'I don't think so,' I said.

Then she found the perfect shoes, a pair of trainers just like my Converse but they were blue and glittery and exactly the same colour as my dress. I was sold. With a silver clutch bag bought online, all I had to find was something to wear on my head.

'I was going to wear my white bandana and daisy chains.'

'You can't wear that, you need something elegant.'

'Elegant. You're the one who told me I could wear Converse!' I said and we both started laughing.

Once I had my outfit sorted, I started to get a bit excited about prom night. Around school all the talk was who would be wearing what and how they were getting there. Most people were hiring stretch limos to ride to the venue in style.

'Don't worry, I'll book a combine harvester,' said Mum.

'I don't think so,' I said.

As prom night got closer, it seemed less likely that Nathan Sykes would be taking me. But my brother Luke said he would take me. I didn't think it would be his thing, as he's twenty and would have to spend the night with a bunch of sixteen-year-olds. But he said he would be honoured to escort me. He's a real gentleman.

The big day arrived. Mum had made an appointment for me to have false eyelashes at a beauty salon in Bexhill. I don't have eyelashes of my own and wanted to have individual lashes as I thought they would look more natural. But when the beautician started putting them on, the glue began to sting my eyes. So we decided I would go for the fake ones. The trouble was they were really long and looked a bit spidery. Mum was panicking as she thought I would end up looking like a drag queen, but I looked so different. It was strange but cool having lashes. I could see them out of the corner of my eye and I couldn't stop blinking.

At home Mum and Ruby helped me get ready. My clothes were all laid out on my bed. Mum's friend Amie dabbed a tiny bit of blue eye shadow on my eyelids and used a cotton bud to blend it in, while Mum painted my fingernails blue to match my dress. Then she sewed the back of my dress to stop it falling down. 'I should have bought a couple of chicken fillets,' I joked.

Outside the house a big shiny grey Bentley pulled up on the drive. My brother Luke stepped out, he looked so smart in his grey suit. Mum and Dad took loads of photos, and then Dad picked me up out of my wheelchair and carried me into the passenger seat of the Bentley. I felt like a celebrity. Everyone was taking photos. Our neighbour came out to wave me off and started crying. I think that was a good thing! I hope it was.

Outside the hotel, Mum and Dad were waiting for me with my wheelchair. While I waited for Courtney, I watched the other kids arrive. One dude turned up on top of a camper van on a surf board wearing a wig. It was hilarious. Someone actually turned up on a tractor - sitting on the front in the shovel. That was the coolest entrance I've ever seen. Courtney arrived looking so pretty. She usually wears her hair straight, but she had it all curled. She looked all grown up.

Inside we all sat at our tables. I sat between Courtney and Luke while the dinner was served. We had melon chunks, strawberries and grapes to start followed by a chicken thing with mushrooms and white wine sauce. It looked disgusting so I didn't even bother to try it. Dessert was a chocolate mousse thing which was OK, but it was dark chocolate and I prefer white or milk chocolate. Luckily I sneaked a Milky Way Crispy Roll chocolate bar into my clutch bag, so I ate that instead. After dinner they presented the awards. We had all been given forms to vote for things like Rear of the Year, the Biggest Heartbreaker, Biggest Flirt, Cutest Couple, Everybody's Friend, Comedian of the Year, Biggest Legend and Biggest Liability. I didn't pay much attention as I hadn't bothered voting. If I had I would have voted myself as the Biggest Liability. Then the DJ started playing music. It was mostly chart and dub music, which I hate. There was lots of stupid dancing going on. Luke is a really good break-dancer, so I made him get up and do The Worm. Everyone was watching him and I just sat there and tapped my leg. Even If I wasn't in a wheelchair, I wouldn't have got up to dance.

One of the girls from our year who doesn't usually speak to me saw Luke and came up to talk to us, which was kind of awkward. She sat with us the whole night, flirting.

'You do realise she has this massive thing for you,' I whispered to Luke.

He has a girlfriend and wasn't interested, which made it even more hilarious. Just as the slow dances started and all the boys started asking girls to dance, my dad turned up to take me home, which was a relief. I hadn't expected the prom to be such fun, but it was.

The following day I checked Twitter and there was a DM from Nathan.

'Hey U! So sorry I couldn't make it yesterday! You looked adorable and I really wish I could of (sic) been there!! Sad face. See you soon! Xx.'

I was so happy, tears rolled down my face.

Chapter 9

'Music, Magic and Ghosts'

The things that make me happy and sometimes sad

I do watch a lot of TV, and I mean a lot, but I also learn a lot from it. My dad says you can get some good knowledge from programmes on the Discovery Science channel. One of our favourites is *How It's Made*. I like it when you see how they melt old bits of metal down to make iron bars and stuff. 'Do they really do it like that?' I ask, because it looks too hot and dangerous to be true. Other times they go to factories and show the people working there, doing these really boring jobs putting things in boxes.

'I don't know how they can do that all day,' I say. 'But they seem happy enough, they're always smiling.'

'I think that's something to do with the camera being there,' Dad says.

I like to share what I've learnt on TV with my friends. At school Courtney used to call it Hayley's life facts because I would always be coming out with scientific stuff I had learnt off TV the night before. I also like to learn about how things work and the way people used to do things hundreds of years ago. My dad and I always watch programmes about Ancient Egypt and the pyramids or people finding bunkers from the war. I find history on TV really interesting, but the way it is taught in school, copying facts and dates out of books, is so boring.

The programme *Breaking Magic* is cool. They show you how magic tricks are done by using science. One of the presenters is a girl called Billy who does all kinds of really clever stuff. In one trick I watched she went to a boxing gym to see if her mental powers could beat strength. She told the boxers 'I can take away all of your strength' and they laughed at her. Then she told one of the boxers to sit on a chair. She put her hand on his chest and asked him to get up and he did. Then she put her thumb on his forehead and told him to get up, but he couldn't. He was a huge boxer and she was only tiny, but he struggled to get up and fell backwards off his chair. After the trick they explained it was all about centre of gravity not strength. To stand up a person needs to lean forward and place their centre of gravity over their feet. When Billy put her hands on his chest the boxer was still able to shift but when she put her thumb on his forehead she kept his centre of gravity behind his feet and as he pushed against her thumb his weight fell backwards toward his centre of gravity and he toppled over. It was so clever.

In another programme Billy and another presenter took a group of people to a haunted asylum. There was a load of patient records there and they asked one of the guys in the group to pass them the file labelled J, which was the records of a patient who they said had an unhealthy obsession with starting fires. When the presenter started reading through the file, the paper burst into flames and everyone was shocked. Then the presenter pulled down a projector screen and started showing them a picture and that burst into flames as well. Everyone was scared and told to leave the building. I would have been scared if I had been in the room with them too. But there was a scientific explanation for the supernatural. I learnt that it was caused by a chemical called white phosphorus which burns when it gets into contact with oxygen in the air. To slow the reaction down they had mixed it with another chemical called carbon disulphide, and then poured the mixture on to pages of the file before closing it. When the file was opened the disulphide evaporated and the white phosphorus mixed with oxygen and caught fire. The same happened when they unrolled the projector screen. It was really cool.

Come Dine With Me is another of my favourite programmes. Every week four strangers invite people round to their house and cook them dinner, then they have to vote which one is best and the winner gets £1,000. At one point I had fifty episodes on our TV planner, so I spent a whole day in front of the TV watching back-to-back episodes. I love the commentator, Dave Lamb. Even though you only ever hear his voice, he is the star of the show. His comments are so sarcastic and hilarious. I think we could be best friends. But I would never want to take part in the show because I hate trying new food. I would be the fussy person that everyone hates. So I just watch.

Mum and I like watching *Ghost Adventures* with Zak Bagans. In each show a team of American guys go ghost hunting and get locked in places that are supposed to be haunted. Mum and Courtney think the presenter Zak is really fit, but he's really old. He's like thirty-seven, almost as old as Mum. It would be so cool to meet them. Mum says that there used to be an old asylum on the site where my Auntie Janie's house is built. All that's left of it is a brick wall, which really creeps me out. Maybe I'll write to Zak Bagans and invite him to Auntie Janie's. I think Mum would like to be locked in a haunted house with Zak.

When I was five or six I used to be obsessed with the crocodile hunter Steve Irwin. I would shout 'crikey' at the TV whenever I watched his programmes. Once Mum arranged with the TV show *This Morning* for me to meet him at an animal park in Kent. It was such a surprise I really did shout 'crikey'. Now I love watching survival guy Bear Grylls. He's not hot or anything, but I think he would be such a good mate to have. If I was ever lost anywhere I would just call Bear Grylls. People always say, 'If you were stuck on a desert island, what three things would you take with you?' Everyone usually answers food, water and shelter. But I would take a boat. That way I could get off the island. That's the logical answer.

Logical is quite a long word, isn't it? I like using long words, trying to make myself sound clever when really I'm not. One of my favourite words is peasant. I thought it was a type of bird until Courtney said, 'I think you mean pheasant.' So I'm not really as clever as I like to think. Another word I like using is pretentious. They use it all the time on *Come Dine With Me*, especially if they write their menu in French or something and the presenter says 'that's pretentious'. I asked Mrs G what pretentious means and she said it means trying to be posh and clever. So I can sound pretentious by saying pretentious and that's pretentious in itself.

Discombobulated is another good word to drop into a conversation. I first heard it when Nathan from The Wanted tweeted to say he was discombobulated. I googled it and found out it means confused. I once asked a teacher what it meant and she didn't know, so I had to explain it to her. Now I like using it just to confuse people.

My greatest passion in the whole world is music. I love bands as I've already mentioned, and you'll learn more later. But I also have my quiet moments when I sit down with a good book. My favourite books at the moment are the *Twilight* series and *The Vampire Diaries*. I've finished reading *The Hunger Games* by Suzanne Collins. In case you've just landed from another planet and never heard of them, they are three books set in the future. These kids have to appear on a live TV show called 'The Hunger Games' where the only rule is 'kill or be killed.' In the first book the main character Kat has a little sister who becomes a nurse. She was supposed to be in the Hunger Games but Kat volunteered to take her place and survived. After I'd finished reading the book, I watched the film, and then carried on reading the next book *Catching Fire*. When I got to the final book, *Mockingjay,* I didn't want it to end. It was so sad. I have never cried at a book before, but it made me so sad. I felt like I really connected with the characters so much. Spoiler alert – in the end Prim died - it was really sad. Now I can't wait to see the film, I know I'm going to cry.

Although I really enjoy cooking and watching TV programmes about cooking, I am really fussy with my food, which is a bit weird. As a baby I was what the midwife called 'a grazer', meaning I would eat little and often. I haven't changed that much, I still eat lots of little meals rather than a plate full. At home I only ever eat cereals, potatoes or toast, with loads of butter. Whenever we go out to eat as a family, it's usually to our local carvery, and then I'll only eat roast potatoes and gravy. I also like mash, jacket potatoes and new potatoes, but I make Mum take the skins off.

I've enjoyed cooking ever since I was little and used to spend weekends with my Nanna and Pops. One of my early memories is helping Nanna to make flapjacks and gingerbread men or chocolate cakes. In GCSE lessons we would sometimes cook using Jamie Oliver recipes for lemon butter biscuits and chocolate brownies or chicken curry and naan bread. Mum says I make a 'wicked' chocolate brownie. For my GCSE exam I made rainbow cupcakes, which were the best things I've ever cooked. I found the recipe on the internet, it was really simple. All I had to do was make normal cake mix, then divide it into six different bowls and mix in red, purple, blue, yellow, green, and orange food colouring. Then I put a layer of each colour into a cupcake case and cooked them like normal cupcakes. When I took them out of the oven, they looked and smelt like normal cupcakes, but when you bit into them all the coloured layers looked like a rainbow. Yum. I took them home and everyone ate them, which is quite rare. Even Mum said they were nice.

As part of my GCSE food technology course I had to do lots of different things with cheesecakes. One week we concentrated on doing something different with the base, so I used chocolate chips. Then we had to try something different with the topping, using different flavours each week. Mum reckoned we had cheesecakes coming out of our ears by the time that part of the course finished. Usually, if I make cake, I like to scrape every last bit of the mixture out of the bowl. The teacher used to think it was because I didn't like wasting food but actually I was just being lazy to save on washing up.

In 2012 I was asked if I would like to take part in a charity cookbook called the *Celebrity Bake Book*, which was put together to raise money for a charity called the Ben Kinsella Trust. There were loads of famous people off the TV like Jamie Oliver, Fearne Cotton, Mary Berry from the 'Great British Bake Off' and Lorraine Kelly, who I met a couple of times when I went to London for the Children of Achievement Awards. It was weird to be asked because I'm not really a celebrity or anything, but I gave them a recipe for fairy cakes which was really easy to make.

I know lots of useful cookery tips. Mostly I've learnt them the hard way. For starters, never rub chilli in your eyes. I know because my eye started to itch once when I was once in the middle of making a Thai green curry. It really, really stung and my eyes started to water. The smell of garlic is also really hard to get off your clothes, so never wipe your fingers in your jumper when you're making spaghetti bolognese. I also discovered that when a glass is full you really should stop pouring! This happened when I was making lemonade in school. I was pouring it from a jug and I don't know what went wrong with my brain, but I kept on pouring when there was no more room in the glass. I said to myself, 'What are you doing?' It was so hilarious – I was laughing so much I made myself cry. Afterwards I was quite embarrassed; I had to sit in the middle of the class with a warm, wet, lemony lap. It wasn't very nice.

In food technology lessons at school, I made loads of different things like butternut-squash risotto, cheese straws, cheese and onion pasties, apple pie, chicken burgers, seafood spaghetti, vegetable curry, rice pudding, banoffee pie and chocolate-and-cherry cheesecake (one of Mum's particular favourites). Mostly I took the cakes and sweet things home for Mum, and Dad would eat the spicy food. He used to look forward to Wednesday evenings. He said my Thai green curry was a 'winner'. I like to think of it as my speciality. I have made it a few times and Dad always says it's delicious. It's weird: I can make a Thai green curry but I can't cook a piece of toast.

Not all my cooking has been a success. I don't know what went wrong with my bread rolls but they went straight in the bin when I got home. 'You could smash windows with those,' Mum said.

I didn't quite get the coleslaw right either. I think I might have used too much yoghurt, but Mum took one look in the container, said it was 'slop' and that went the same way as the bread rolls.

Backstage with my favourite band, The Wanted (2012)

With Blue Peter TV presenter Helen Skelton (2011)

Me and Louis behind the scenes at Fox 25 News (2014). And (below) with American TV presenter Barbara Walters (2009)

With Harry Crowther and his mum Sharron at the
Masquerade Ball (2012)

Photo by Jason Fry Photography

Best friends forever: me and Courtney (2009)

My good luck card from Mrs G (below)

Signing copies of my book *Old Before My Time* at Waterstones, Eastbourne. Below, me and Mum, watching my book off the press at CPI Mackays printers in Chatham (2011)

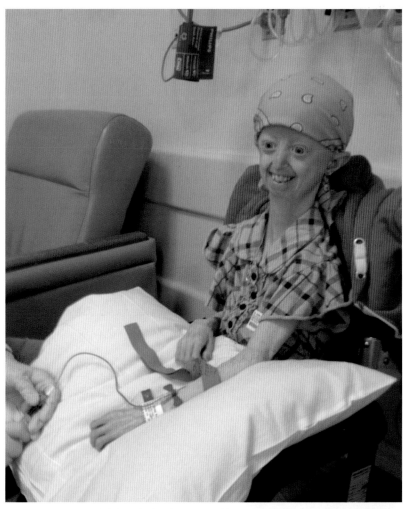

How much blood do they need?
Boston (2014)

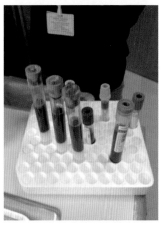

Me and Lindsay, my drug-trial partner (2014)

With Dr Leslie Gordon from the Progeria Research Foundation
(2009)

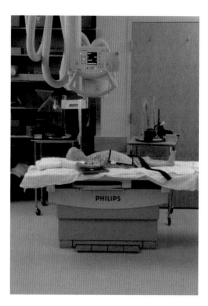

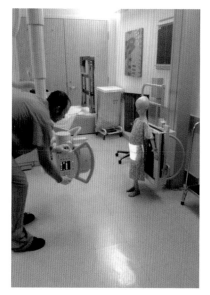

Scans, scans and more scans at
Boston Children's Hospital (2014)

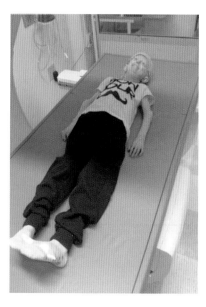

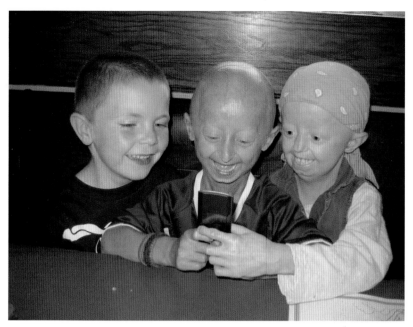

Louis, Michiel and me (2007)

Sam Berns' dad Scott with Mum, Louis and me taking part in
the Progeria Research Foundation's Race for Research
in Boston (2007)

My heart will go on: sightseeing in Boston (2007)

Me and Dad in Denmark (2014)

At the Reunion in Italy with my friend Claudia
Photo by Jason Fry Photography

And, below, with a giant bug (2012) Photo by Benno Neeleman

With my mum at Port Lympne Zoo in Kent during the Progeria Reunion (2010)

A day out in Denmark (2014)

Me and Harry congratulate my sister Charlotte, far right, and Becky, left, at the end of their Ten-in-Ten marathon (2012)

Me and Charlotte at a fund-raising Zumba night (2011)

Following the leader: Harry, Louis and me at the Progeria Reunion in Denmark (2014)

With Jesper, left, and Claudia, right, at the Progeria Reunion in Ashford, Kent (2013) Photo by Jason Fry Photography

They're playing our song; Michiel and I have the last dance at the
Progeria Reunion in Denmark (2014)

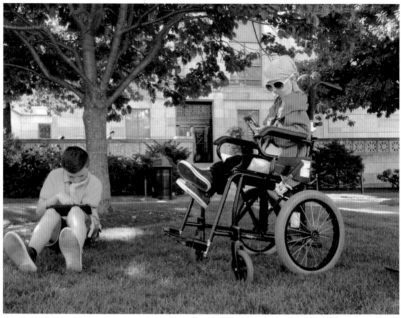

Me and Louis looking all studious at Harvard University in Boston (2014)

Sisters in arms: me and Ruby (2011)

Chapter 10

'The Easiest £120 I'll Ever Earn'

Or the day I got my GCSE results

August 21 2014: GCSE Results Day.

I was three thousand miles away being tested for the drug trials in Boston and stressing about my grades. Back home in Bexhill, I had given Mum permission to go to school and pick up my results but first I made her promise not to tell anyone, or put anything out on Facebook, before telling me. I know what she's like! I had been offered a place at Bexhill College to do media studies and needed a C in both English and maths. I have no idea why, but I was so nervous.

Mum had said that for every grade I got higher than hers she would give me £10 and her friend offered to double it to £20. 'This is going to be the easiest £120 I'll ever earn.' I thought, as Mum only got Ds and Es in her exams. She had a D in typing. I mean what's all that about? That's not even a proper subject, is it?

I was really hoping to get a good grade in maths as I didn't want to have to resit it in college. My Pops said we could build a bonfire and burn all my maths books, so I swotted loads for my exams. I spent hours and hours in school with Mrs G, going over revision books and hundreds of test papers. Then, as the exams got closer, I worked on my own at home. There was no point in asking my mum for help, because she is rubbish at equations and percentages. And anyway, I thought, I can't ask anyone to help me in the exam so I've just got to figure it out for myself.

I had to sit two papers in maths, one with and one without a calculator, three English exams and a written exam in food technology. I also had a practical exam in art. When it came to sitting the written exams, I got another of my Progeria perks. I was allowed to sit in a room on my own, with Mrs G, while the rest of the school had to sit their exams in the sports hall. My friend Courtney was so jealous?

'Why do you get special treatment?' she asked.

'Because my stomach makes funny noises when it's quiet and it's really embarrassing.'

There was no way I could still for an hour and forty-five minutes without annoying the other kids around me. Plus I was allowed to use a laptop to write my English exams because my hands are so weak I can't write long essays.

The actual exams weren't as scary as I thought they were going to be. I quite enjoyed the art exam because most of it was practical and based around the theme of order and disorder. So I had been out taking photographs with my Dad throughout the year and for the final practical we had to create something that represented order and disorder. I decided to make a hat for the Mad Hatter from *Alice in Wonderland* because I thought, 'well he's mad, and that's a good example of disorder'. I made a tube and cut circles out of cardboard and splattered it with paint. I couldn't believe it took me two days to make it, but I was quite pleased when it was finished. My food-tech exams were mostly practical, too, but I had to sit a written exam. I had to answer questions like, why do they have to test food in a clean environment? I was so tempted to write because otherwise they will get a disease and die. But the actual answer I wrote was really posh and used long words: 'to ensure they don't catch unwanted diseases or bacteria'. I used the world ensure, as I thought that would get me a mark even if the rest of the answer was wrong.

The maths exam was a different story. When I opened my first maths paper I thought: 'This is a great start. I don't even understand the first question!' It was all in a foreign language to me. I just sat there for what seemed like forever, but was only a couple of minutes, and my mind went blank. Then I gave myself a good talking to.

'Don't panic, just move on to something you do know.'

The next question was a stem-and-leaf diagram, which was easy. Now I know you're probably thinking, what on earth is a stem-and-leaf diagram? Well I'm not very good at explaining things, that's why I wouldn't make a good teacher, but they are diagrams where you put lots of numbers and information on a chart and answer questions about them. My question was all to do with foreign currencies and exchange rates. As I have travelled to lots of different places across the world, I got it straight away. Some of the questions about percentages, graphs and volumes and areas were easy. But as I got further into the paper, the questions got harder. Simultaneous equations, circumferences of circles, angles of triangles. I thought, 'what's the point?' Some of the questions were really stupid and I started to get mad, thinking they must be trick questions. One question asked if a small bottle of water costs 78p for 60cl and a large bottle costs £1.99 for 150cl, what is the best value for money? I wanted to answer 'Do your own shopping?' But I thought I wouldn't get extra marks for sarcasm, so I just guessed and hoped for the best.

At 6 a.m. on the morning of the GCSE results day, I was lying in bed in my hotel in Boston thinking, 'Don't get stressed. It's not important. As long as you pass English and maths you can go to college.' Suddenly my phone buzzed and there was Mum's face on Facetime. I couldn't tell if she was looking happy or disappointed.

'I went up to the school and they wouldn't give me your results,' she said.

'Great!' I thought. All that stress for nothing.

'The school said I had to have a signed letter from you, before they would give them out. But I told them you were in Boston and I refused to leave. After speaking to the exam board and three different teachers, they finally gave in.'

'Well?'

There was a long pause. I could see the corners of Mum's mouth were twitching as if she was finding it hard not to smile.

'You got five Cs. Well done'

'What about maths?'

'A D. Never mind.'

No! I was really annoyed with myself, knowing that I would have to resit maths when I started in college, but I was happy I had passed. I will just have to wait another year before lighting that bonfire for my maths books.

Chapter 11

'I'm Such a Twitter Monster'

My life through social media

You could say I'm a bit obsessed with Twitter; from the moment I wake up until the time I go to sleep I'm on it. I guess that's another typical teenager thing. I'll tweet like twenty times a day: pictures of my favourite boy band, cute animal photos, things that make me laugh and pictures of our dogs being stupid. People who follow me on Twitter mostly know me as a fan girl. I think most people on Twitter know I have Progeria but no one says anything. I am who I am. I don't act any different from how I do in real life. People know I'm seventeen and they don't talk to me like I'm a kid, which is cool. I like that.

My Twitter name is @hayleyokinesx. There is another person on there pretending to be me who calls themselves @QueenHay-Ley. She says she is thirteen and 'has the rare aging disease that don't make her any different'. Her profile picture is a photo of me when I met Willow Smith back in 2011. She has 2558 followers and Tweets things like, 'It makes me happy when everyone say nice things about me!' and, 'deep inside I am no different from anyone! We are all human.' Seriously it's not me. I don't even know why these people bother, it's just weird. You can tell that I am who I say I am on Twitter because I change my profile picture all the time depending on how bored I get. It's usually a photo of me with one of my favourite bands or a band member. Currently I have a photo of me with The Wanted, but I will probably change it soon.

I mostly follow bands and friends on Twitter and even a few celebrities. I have more than 7,500 followers. I used to have more but some people have unfollowed me because I didn't follow them back.

Have I mentioned that my favourite person in the world, Nathan Sykes, who was in The Wanted, is following me? The day I saw him on my account I actually cried, I was so happy. I tweeted, 'Nathan Sykes is one big bag of adorable' with a smiley face.

There are a lot of people on Twitter who dislike me for a lot of reasons. I would, too, if I weren't me, because I speak my mind and I'm pretty honest about people that I don't like. I seem to turn into this Twitter monster because I know that no one can smack me, when really if the person was standing next to me I would I just say 'sorry'. In the past I have got myself into loads of arguments. If someone is annoying me I'll say, 'Will you just shut up please. No one cares what you're saying.' Then their friends get involved and these people who I have never spoken to before start being horrible to me. So Courtney feels she has step in to calm the situation down. She'll say, 'Hayley has her opinion, you have your opinion just leave it there.' I am trying to calm down on Twitter, but it's difficult when people are always moaning about stupid things. Sometimes I feel like some comments are aimed at me, even though I know they are not. I've never had any death threats or anything really bad, but One Direction fans can be vicious. I try not to say anything about them anymore, it's too dangerous.

Mostly I like to share the things I'm doing and how I'm feeling. I share things with everyone, not many people care, but I share all the same. My Twitter account is like having a best friend with you all the time. When I'm mad with Mum I'll tweet things followed by lots of angry red faces.

Here are just some of my Tweets, to give you an idea how random I can be:

- 'The Vampire Diaries almost made me cry again but I couldn't because my auntie was next to me'
- 'Nothing more upsetting than realising you only have 3 Magic Stars left when you thought you had more'
- 'Have you ever had a dream that's so heartbreaking that when you wake up you're actually crying?' (That was actually about a really sad, but embarrassing dream I had I about the drummer from the band 5SOS)
- 'Just killed a fly with rolled up newspaper on the first try I'm pretty proud of myself'
- 'Only good thing about getting a McDonald's now is I got

one of those caramel iced frappé things yum'

- 'I have my showers so hot my skin goes red is that normal?'

Twitter is also good for meeting new people. I've started talking to a new friend called Shannon. She lives in Cambridgeshire and is a year younger than me. I first 'met' her as she had one of my favourite Twitter accounts. I used to check her tweets every day because she loved the band 5 Seconds of Summer or 5SOS. It's a fact but before we started talking I was scared of her. Well, scared might be a bit dramatic, but I was intimidated because she had thousands of followers and I'm so awkward.

I was 'stalking' her account one day when I noticed something. I tweeted 'Don't mean to alarm you but do you know you have 666 followers ', and sent her a screen shot and told her that she was one of my favourite accounts on Twitter. When she didn't reply I thought, 'Great, now she thinks I'm a weirdo.' Then one day, when I wasn't expecting it, she tweeted back 'No way!' It turned out that we both used to read each other's tweets every day and were both a bit obsessed with the band 5SOS . We are planning to meet in person when we go to their concert next year. I can't wait.

Chapter 12

'Our Exclusive Club'

Or what we really get up to at the Progeria Reunions

Having progeria is like being in a really exclusive club and once a year we all get together somewhere in the world at the Progeria Reunions. Over the years Mum, Dad and I have met people who have become some of our closest friends. It's like one big holiday. We get taken out on day trips, go to see lots of cool places and party like no one's watching. For a couple of days, we are all the same, there's no one to ask what's wrong?

Our first Sunshine Progeria Reunion was in Washington DC. I was only three so don't remember too much about it, but we have lots of old photos of me, Mum, Dad and my sisters Charlotte and Stacey on the plane on the way to America. It was the first time I'd ever been to another country. It was there I met my best friend Maddie. Hers was one of the twenty-seven families invited. At the time there were only forty kids with progeria in the world that we knew of. Everywhere we went the TV news cameras followed us. It's mad because now there are about ninety-four cases. Mum says it's because there is more information about progeria on TV and the internet, so more parents and doctors know what to look for. But TV cameras and reporters still like to follow us around.

Mum used to say that when she first saw all us progeria kids bobbing about in the swimming pool with our bald heads, we looked like boiled eggs in a saucepan.

Over the years we've been to reunions in Florida, Holland, Italy, Denmark, Germany and Turkey and met loads of really nice people. There's Marjet and Klaus from Holland, who started the Progeria Family Circle after their son Ben passed away, Leslie and Scott from the Progeria Research Foundation and Michiel, my friend from Belgium. I used to pair up with Michiel and his parents Wim and Godlieve Vandeweert for the drug trials in Boston for the first couple of years. Michiel is sixteen. Mum says we used to look like 'two peas in a pod' which I always thought was an odd thing to say as we weren't green. Although I 'm sure I turned a funny colour the first time I saw all the needles and injections we had to have. Mum and Dad used to feel really sorry for Michiel's parents because when they found out he had progeria they weren't going to have any more kids. But the doctors said there was like a one in eight million chance of it happening again, so they had a baby sister for Michiel and called her Amber. Then Amber got sick and they found out she had progeria and that really sucks.

Every year when I come back home after a Reunion I think always think it was the best ever. It's hard to pick a favourite. I suppose it's a bit like asking Mum to choose who she likes best out of me, Ruby and Louis. I used to have really good fun when we went to the ones in Florida, because it was always sunny. For a couple of years Mum and Dad organised the Reunions in the UK, which was nowhere near as exciting – or as sunny. It was loads of fun for the other families, but it was really stressful for Mum and Dad who had to raise thousands of pounds to make it happen. Mum blamed the stress of organising the first one for her divorce from Dad. But they still did it again and again. They had to work really hard to book hotels for all the families from Europe to come and stay and then find things for the families to do.

One time Mum's friend Amie and I organised a Masquerade Ball to raise money. It was an idea I had when we came back from a Reunion in Italy where I bought a really cool black and white porcelain mask. Masked balls are a really big thing in Venice. I really wanted to go to a carnival in Venice and wear my mask but it was the wrong time of year. So I thought it would be fun to have our own carnival. Amie booked a ballroom at a hotel near Bexhill and sorted out the food and tickets and everything, and I helped her with the planning and the decorations. We sold a couple of hundred tickets and everyone dressed in their ball gowns, dinner suits and masks. I wore a red satin dress and everyone said I looked like the 'belle of the ball'.

At our first UK Reunion in 2010, there were fifteen other families.

My Auntie Janie and big sister Charlotte helped out looking after all the families and made sure no one was left out. There were two other British families: Ashanti's from London and Harry and his family from Yorkshire. It was the first time Harry had ever been to a Reunion and he made us all laugh with his Michael Jackson impressions. There were four families from Italy, three from Belgium including Michiel and Amber, two from Germany and one each from the Netherlands, Denmark, Portugal and France. Some mums and dads come even if their children have passed on, I suppose it helps them remember the nice things. Sometimes we meet new people like Miles from Sweden - we call him 'Smiles' because he is always grinning. He is the happiest person I know and so cute. Seeing the younger kids at the Reunions remind me of when I was younger and ran around like crazy.

One year all the children worked on putting on a show for the final night called *The Garden of Dreams*. A woman from a dance school helped us put the show together and taught us different song and dance routines. It was set in a magic fairy kingdom and I was the Fairy Queen, who made everyone's dreams come true. So I got to wear a gorgeous white gown and huge wings. The other kids dressed up as fairytale characters from their different countries and had to pretend they had been asleep for thousands of years. It was so much fun as I went around the stage waving my magic wand over everyone, one by one, and making their dreams come true, while Michiel sang, 'Wake up, wake up and follow me to the Garden of Dreams.' Harry, Michiel and a couple of the boys wanted to be breakdancers and made everyone laugh with their moonwalking. Jesper from Denmark was really funny doing the Macarena, and Amber, who was dressed up as Snow White, danced like a real fairy and blew kisses to the parents. At the end of the play Michiel made everyone cry when he sang, 'You'll never walk alone.' It wasn't that Michiel was a bad singer, we were just sad to say goodbye. I try not to think about it too much, but the mums and dads worry about what will have happened in a year's time.

The following year Mum and Dad arranged the Reunion for the autumn. The only trouble with having a Reunion in Ashford in October is the weather. It rained, so most of the activities had to be indoors. We carved pumpkins and made glitter tattoos in the day, and at night we dressed up for a Halloween party. I bought a pair of black angel wings and I was going to dress up as a fallen angel. But I dislocated my hip and wasn't able to walk around, so I thought there would be no point in wearing wings if I had to sit in my chair all night. Instead Mum helped me to backcomb my wig and spray it with glitter so that it looked like I had real scary hair – and I wore loads of make-up and tattoos to look really frightening! At the party my Portuguese friend Claudia made me cry. She doesn't speak much English and I don't speak any Portuguese, but she is the same age and we always dance and play together. She asked me to dance to 'Someone Like You' by Adele. I got up out of my chair but I burst into tears when Claudia started singing to me. I don't know why it made me cry, but it did.

I guess if you were to ask me now what my favourite Reunion is I would say Denmark because it was so different from anywhere I had been before and it's the latest one. Before the Reunion I didn't know very much about Denmark, except that it was the place where Lego was invented. I was expecting everyone to be wearing jumpers and riding around on bicycles as that's what I'd read about on the internet. The Reunion was organised by Jesper Sorensen and his mum Jette. Jesper is sixteen and is the only person in Denmark with progeria, so he's quite famous. Mum and Dad had some money left over in the bank from the last UK Reunion, so they were able to pay for all the families in the UK to fly out. We all met up at the airport. Harry and his family had come from Yorkshire and Mia and Ashanti came from London. Lucy and her family were supposed to fly over from Northern Ireland, but she was not well, so they didn't turn up. The Reunion was held in a place called Rebild Bakker, which means Rebild Hills, near where Jesper and his family live. It's a big national park, with lots of green fields and trees. It was August, so the weather was really warm. We visited lots of great places. One day we were taken to a place called Robber Camp, which I thought sounded a bit dangerous. Turns out I was right. Set up in the middle of the woods, we had quite a long walk to get there. On the way our guide told us stories about highwaymen who used to hide in the forest and when ordinary people rode past they would rob them. 'Charming!' I thought. At the camp there were lots of old-fashioned activities like archery and long-sawing. Dad and Louis took each end of this long saw and cut through a tree trunk. Then they tried axe throwing. The guides showed them how to hold the axe above their shoulder and aim it at a target. Everyone tried except me. Mum tried to get me to join in but I said, 'That axe scares me. I think I'll stay back here and take pictures, thank you very much.' I wouldn't have been able to lift the axe myself so I would never be able to throw it.

On our last night in Denmark, Michiel was DJ-ing. He's a good DJ and has his own radio show in Belgium. I've tried listening but I can't understand what he's saying as I don't speak Flemish. Anyway Michiel decided to play 'Angels' by Robbie Williams. We had danced together to it the previous year. As the song started, he walked towards me across the dance floor with his arms spread out wide. I held out my arms and started crying, I couldn't help myself. As Michiel hugged me on the dance floor I'm pretty sure everyone around us was crying too. I've a feeling that's going to be our song.

Chapter 13

'Ten in Ten'

Why I'm so proud of my marathon-running sister

Before she had her baby, my sister Charlotte was into running. She was always out sprinting around the forests near where she lives with her super-fit friend Becky Reid. One day, out of nowhere, she said, 'Why don't we have a go at this marathon business and run ten marathons in ten days?'

That's like 268 miles, which is just ridiculous.

'That's an awesome idea,' my Dad said. 'But have you run a marathon?'

'Well, um ... not really. But I've run a half marathon and the other day I ran eighteen miles. And I've got a couple of months to get into shape.'

Charlotte wanted to do something to help Mum and Dad when they were raising money to hold the Progeria Reunion in Britain. Because Charlotte has always been close to the other progeria families, she wanted to make sure all the families had a good time. She saw how stressed out Mum and Dad had been working really hard to raise £17,500 to make it all happen so, when they said they were going to do it all over again, she came up with her crazy idea to raise money.

Her friend Becky got out a map and started to plan a route that would take them from Yorkshire, where my friend Harry and his family live, all the way back home to the south of England. They called it the '10 in 10/When Harry Met Hayley' run. Dad volunteered to be their back-up driver and follow them in the car, carrying their bags and water, looking out and just being there for them.

So Charlotte started training. For months she ran everywhere. At the time she was working as a cleaner, so instead of driving from one house to the next, she would run. She ran in the forest. She ran on tracks. She ran along the promenade. She even ran along busy roads where no one in their right mind would think of running. We nicknamed her Forrest Gump. Total strangers would see her running up and down the roads and ask her what she was doing and when she told them, they gave her money, which was kind of nice of them. She set up a site on the internet where people could sponsor her and told as many people as she could think of. Mum and Dad, Harry's family and all our friends told all their friends, and her local newspaper ran a story about her challenge.

As the day of the run got nearer, I thought, 'Wow, she's really going to do this.'

'You're mad', I told her.

She said 'I know. But I can't really do anything to help you with your progeria, so the least I can make sure you and all your friends meet up and spend time together', which I thought was sweet.

It's weird because when I was first diagnosed with progeria and Mum and Dad thought I would not reach my thirteenth birthday, Charlotte had a tough time dealing with it. She was only a teenager herself and tried to block out what might happen. Once she told me, 'A big sister is meant to protect her little brothers and sisters, but with you there was just nothing I could do to make your situation any better.' I didn't understand at the time but now I have a younger brother and sister, I so get it. Like the time when Louis hurt his knee, it made me sad to see him in pain. I would hate it if Ruby or Louis had to go through all the needles and tests I have to.

Finally the big day arrived: Thursday April 5th 2012. Dad drove me, Louis and Ruby up to Yorkshire to meet Charlotte and Becky and we all booked into a hotel the night before. As we got closer to Harry's house in Mirfield, Dad said, 'Look, there's snow', and pointed up towards the Yorkshire Dales where the tops of the mountains were white.

'What if it's snowing tomorrow? Will they still run?' I asked.

'Of course they will,' said Dad. 'They're not going to let a bit of cold weather stop them.'

I thought it might be a bit dangerous running in the snow; they could fall over or something.

The following morning, we all met at Harry's house for the start. It was really lucky that the sun was shining. Harry's dad,

John Crowther, came out wearing running gear too. They were all wearing bright pink vests with the Progeria Family Circle logo on the front, so people could see why they were doing it. Harry's dad was going to run with his friend. But because he is old – forty-three! – he said he was only going to run the first six miles. A photographer and a camera crew from the local newspaper and TV interviewed Harry's dad and Charlotte. When one of the reporters asked Charlotte how fast she was going to run, she replied, 'We're not really setting ourselves a time target because we don't know how we will feel by day three or four. So, if we end up taking six or seven hours we won't really mind,' which I thought was quite sensible.

The countdown started. We all joined in shouting down 'ten, nine, eight, seven, six, five, four, three, two, one, go!' And they were off down the road and out of sight. Dad bundled us back into the car and we drove ahead. When we met again at a place called Ladybower Reservoir, near Sheffield, Harry's dad and his friend were still with them. They had run the whole marathon, 26.8 miles. He did look shattered though.

'Once I got into it, I didn't want to stop,' he said.

Charlotte and Becky had bright red faces, where the sun had burnt them, which was really weird as it was freezing cold.

'Some of those hills were really steep and I thought the wind was going to blow us off course,' she said as we checked into our hotel.

The Ladybower Inn was next to a place called the Derwent Valley Reservoirs.

'That's where the Dambusters pilots used to train in the Second World War,' Dad told us.

When we asked what the Dambusters were, he explained that in the war they flew over Germany and dropped bombs to blow up the dams and flood the country. That's just typical of my dad, he has a head like an encyclopaedia. I think that's where I must get my interest in life facts.

The following morning, after a good sleep, we said goodbye to Harry and his family and Charlotte and Becky set off on their second marathon that would take them through Derbyshire. We followed behind them in the car again. And so they went on: day after day, mile after mile, every step bringing them closer to home and the end of their challenge. By day three, Mum turned up to drive me, Louis and Ruby back home. So we said our goodbyes, wished Charlotte and Becky luck and left them in Dad's care.

'Phone me every night after you finish running,' I said.

'I will,' she promised.

'Even if you're too tired to hold the phone?'

'I promise.'

And with that they were off again.

'I hope they will be OK,' I said to my dad.

'Course they will. As long as they don't injure themselves, they'll be fine. They're young and fit and have put in loads of training.'

Day six arrived and disaster. Dad called and he sounded a bit worried.

'Charlotte's hit a wall and needs to talk to you.'

'Oh my goodness,' I said. 'Is she all right? Where was the wall?'

Then Dad explained that the 'wall' was something runners say when they can't go any further and I felt embarrassed. He handed the phone to Charlotte and she was really crying.

'I can't go on,' she blubbed.

'Oh dear,' I thought to myself, I'm not very good at sympathy. 'What's wrong?'

'My calf started swelling a couple of days ago. I thought it was just a stress injury and it would go away if I kept running. But it hurts. I can't run any further.'

I didn't really know what to say. She sounded like she was in a bit of a state.

'You know you can do it,' I said, hoping I was saying the right thing. 'Just think of all the money you're going to get and how much fun we'll all have at the Reunion. When you get to the end I'll be there waiting for you with the biggest hug you've ever had.'

That seemed to cheer her up a bit and she stopped blubbing.

'Do your best, I know you're an amazing sister whatever.'

'Is she really OK? She sounds spaced out,' I said to my dad when he came back on the phone.

'She's had a tough couple of days. Her ankle is hurting and she's annoyed with herself for being injured. It's raining and she's tired. Last night she and Becky didn't get much sleep. There was a group of drunks in the hotel, who kept knocking Becky's bedroom door and frightening her. But now that she has spoken to you, she seems a bit happier.'

'Give her a big hug and a kiss from me,' I said.

I was a little bit worried that she was going to do herself some damage. The last thing I wanted was for another member of our family to be crippled.

The final day arrived: 14 April 2012. Mum, Ruby, Louis and I all drove down to Cranbrook where Charlotte and Becky would be ending their run. They had run through snow. Run through rain. Run along busy roads. Run up mountains. Run down hills. They had run through the centre of London and even got lost a few times along the way. Now they were on the last leg, quite literally. When we pulled up outside the Weald Sports Centre there was a group of more than a hundred people waiting for them. The flags were out; balloons with giant figure tens were flying. There was even a chocolate cake with two little runners on top that looked like Becky and Charlotte in their black leggings and pink vests. A news crew from the BBC was waiting to interview them. Dad took me, Louis and Ruby up the road, so we could see them arrive first. Soon I saw their pink jackets in the distance. As they got closer and closer, I could see they were still smiling, which was pretty amazing.

For the final half mile, Charlotte grabbed the handles of my wheelchair and pushed me along. I've never been so scared in all my life. The road was so bumpy; I thought I was going to fall out. I was hanging on and my bones were shaking. It was only a few hundred yards but it felt like a marathon. 'Now I know why I've never liked running,' I thought. As we ran down the road towards the finishing line, the crowd was getting bigger and bigger. There were people lined up on both sides of the road shouting, 'You can do it, keep going.'

'Why did you do it?' a reporter from a local newspaper asked her once she had crossed the finish line.

'I wanted Hayley to be proud of me in the way that I am proud of her,' she said.

'And what kept you going?' asked another reporter.

'You just think what other people have to get up to every morning, and think: "Yes, I can do it."'

That was such a nice thing to say, I felt so proud of her. She had got through it and raised £7,000 to help Mum and Dad pay for the Progeria Reunion.

Then the reporter asked me what I thought of Charlotte.

'I knew she'd be able to do it. I'm ridiculously proud.'

And I was.

Chapter 14

'I Try Not to Think Too Much of What Lies Ahead and Focus on the Happy Times'

On my friends who have passed on

I can't stand it when my dad cries. It scares me. It means something really bad must have happened. The only time I remember actually seeing my dad cry was once when I was younger and he had been arguing with Mum and also when my dog Boo passed away. But that was different because we were all sad for Boo.

One weekend in January 2014, Dad was at our house while Mum has gone to visit her sister. Ruby and I were watching TV in the lounge when I heard him outside in the hallway, whispering to someone on the phone. I couldn't hear what he was saying, but when he came into the lounge, he looked as if he was going to cry.

'You know Sam in America,' he said.

I thought it was a bit of a stupid thing to say. Of course I knew Sam. He lived near Boston and was one of the first kids with progeria I met when we went to the Sunshine Reunion in Florida when I was three. Sam's parents were both doctors, Scott Berns and Leslie Gordon, and they had started the Progeria Research Foundation to find a cure for progeria. It was all down to them that I had been going out to Boston for so many years taking part in the drug trials. Every time we visited Boston we met them. We had seen him the previous January when I went out for my last check up at the Boston Children's Hospital and I was looking forward to seeing them again on our next visit.

Dad sat down on the sofa between me and Ruby and hugged us both.

'Sam's passed away,' he said.

I started to cry a little bit, then Ruby started to cry and I could feel Dad's arms shaking as he held us. I didn't ask how or why. What was the point? When me and Ruby finally stopped crying, Dad went out into the garden. I could see him standing outside on the decking. He didn't know I was watching him, but I could see he was crying. His hand was shaking as he was lighting his fag.

He must have been really scared. I was sacred, too, but I didn't want to say anything that would only worry my family. Sam was seventeen, a year older than I was then and he also had Hutchinson-Gilford progeria. He was a bit like me. Everyone in the little town where he lived, Sharon in Massachusetts knew him. He had been on TV loads of times and he had a film made about him called *Life According to Sam*, which was shown on the HBO TV channel in America and won a bunch of awards. He had met loads of celebrities and was a mascot for his favourite American football team the New England Patriots, just like I had been with Chelsea Football Club. He was always happy. He used to say, 'Be OK with what you can't do because there is so much that you can do.' He always wanted to play drums in his high school marching band but couldn't because the drums were almost as heavy as he was. But he never gave up on his dream. They made him a special lightweight drum which he could carry and he was able to lead the band. Once, when a journalist asked him what was the most important thing people should know about him, he replied 'I have a very happy life.'

Three months before he died, Sam gave a speech to something called a TEDx conference. He was really brave and sat on a stage in front of thousands of people and talked about his philosophy for a happy life. The film is on Youtube and more than 5.5 million people have watched it. It shows Sam as I will remember him most; happy and making people laugh. He said, 'Being brave isn't supposed to be easy, it's the key way to moving forward.' Sam never wasted energy feeling bad for himself; he just surrounded himself with people he wanted to be with and kept moving forward.

'Even though there are many obstacles in my life, with a lot of them being created by progeria, I don't want people to feel bad for me. I don't think about these obstacles all the time and I'm able to overcome most of them anyway,' he said. That's a good philosophy to have in life, I think. His other tip was, 'Never miss a party if you can help it.'

They said Sam died from complications from progeria. Apparently there were people queuing up outside the funeral wanting to say goodbye to him. That same year two other teenage friends passed away both aged fifteen: American Hana Hwang, and Teresa, who lived in Italy and used to come to our European Progeria Reunions. Her best friend Serena passed two years before her. Serena was always happy and smiling and used to say 'ti amo, ti amo' which is Italian for 'I love you'. She was only twelve.

In four years sixteen progeria children from all over the world have passed on. Some I know, others I have never met, but it still makes Mum and Dad sad. When Dean from Birmingham passed away in 2012, Mum was really sad as she had been close to Dean and his family. We first met when I was invited on to the Jeremy Kyle TV show. He said he wanted to meet me and Ashanti, the girl with progeria from London, because he wanted to show us both that you can have a full and happy life. Dean was so cool. He was twenty, had a girlfriend and drove his own car.

Mum went to the funeral, but I stayed home with Dad. I don't like funerals. When my best friend Maddie died, I went to her funeral and gave a speech. I was eight at the time and we were like sisters, so I wanted to go. I remember it didn't feel like a funeral because everyone was wearing pink and purple, which were Maddie's favourite colours. Sometimes I still think about Maddie, but I try not to because it upsets me, so I try to focus on the happy times when we were together. After Boo died, Ruby started saying things like, 'Boo and Maddie are probably having loads of fun together running around, doing crazy things in Heaven', which is sweet.

I try not to think too much of what lies ahead. There's no point, it's too depressing. So I put it out of my mind and get on with my life. I have to think 'I'm healthy and I feel fine.' I go for regular checkups with Dr Whincup so if there was anything bad, it wouldn't be hard to see. I have a healthy heart and my blood vessels are good, so that's how I deal with the future.

Chapter 15

'Science Stuff Just Goes Over My Head'

My diary from the Boston drug trials

I wouldn't say I enjoy going out to Boston every year for the trials and tests, but I'm used to them. I've been going regularly since I was nine years old. At first we used to go every four months, then six months, but now it's once every eighteen months, which is not so bad. I still don't like having needles but the older I get the easier it is. The first couple of times the nurses would miss my vein and have to keep trying. But now they know where to find my best veins. There's a massive one in my left arm. The worst place for having an injection is near my elbow. If they dig into the muscle it hurts like I'm being pinched or something and leaves a bruise, which is not very nice.

The drug trials are held at the Boston Children's Hospital in America and run by Dr Leslie Gordon and the people at the Progeria Research Foundation. They've been working to find a cure for progeria. Right now I'm about to start the fourth round of clinical trials.

Mum is pleased that the trials are going in the right direction. Thinking back to the first time we met Dr Leslie and her son Sam at our first Reunion in 2000, no one even knew what caused progeria. But now Dr Leslie and the people they work with have not only found out what causes it and they are getting closer to finding a cure. I'll try to explain what causes Hutchinson-Gilford progeria in the easiest way I can. Basically everyone makes something called progerin in their cells during their lifetime, which weakens the structure of cells and makes us get old. With progeria there's a mutation in the DNA which makes more progerin than normal so we age eight times faster and we are more likely to have heart attacks and strokes at a young age. Mum and Dad understand it better, when they try to explain things to me; it goes straight in one ear and out the other. The doctors in Boston say progerin is like our body clock is telling us to slow down. Dr Leslie says kids with progeria deserve to live long healthy happy lives by having medicine that cures and takes care of us so we can be happy kids and adults. The doctors and scientists in America are really pleased that they have found what causes progeria and found drugs that are working on it so quickly because they say it's taken a hundred years to find a treatment for children with diabetes. But we are already on the fourth drug trial to try and slow it down. The main drug I have been testing is the FTI, which is easier to say than the proper name: farnesyltransferase inhibitors. The drugs act as a barrier, to stop the progerin from damaging the cells and so slow down the ageing.

When I started the drug trials in America in 2007 I had to have a full body MOT to make sure my body could cope with all the drugs and tests. They measured me and I was 97cm tall and weighed 12kg when most other nine-year-old girls were twice as heavy and 30cm taller. Dad filmed my first ever drug trial on video for my TV documentary *The 96-year-old Schoolgirl*. I was one of twenty-eight kids from sixteen countries taking part. For the first couple of years we used to go out as a family with Mum and Dad and Ruby and Louis and we would meet up with Michiel and his parents from Belgium. But now there are forty-five kids taking part, Michiel goes out with his sister Amber.

It's horrible not having Michiel around, but I have a new friend, Lindsay. Lindsay lives in Michigan, with her family. She is ten and so cute. The very first time we met we all went out for dinner in Boston. Lindsay sat next to me, but she didn't say much all night and I didn't say much to her except hello.

The next day her mum Kristy came up to me and said, 'Lindsay was really nervous about meeting you. She didn't want to say the wrong thing that would make her seem stupid.'

I didn't know what to say.

'She doesn't have to be nervous of me,' I said. 'She wouldn't say the wrong thing and I wouldn't think she was stupid.'

Really I was just as nervous meeting her. Once her mum had broken the ice between us, we got on really well.

She said to me, 'I hope I'm as pretty as you when I am 16.'

Well, I didn't know what to say. It was like meeting a younger version of me.

Whenever we go to Boston we have to keep a log of all my drugs and a food diary, which is basically potato, potato and more potato. Mum used to worry that I wasn't getting enough nutrition when I was little, but she's given up trying to force feed me vegetables and stuff. On the first morning we always wake up really early because our bodies still think they are on UK-time which is five hours ahead. It's really confusing!

One time when I went with Mum and Auntie Janie, they thought it would be funny to wake me up in the worst way by opening the windows, turning on all the lights, ripping the covers off my bed and shouting 'wake up' in my ear. What they didn't realise is that made me want to stay in bed even longer. Then they moaned at me all day for being in a bad mood. I warned them, 'If you wake me up like that again I will just go back to sleep and I will not wake up – ever.' So she doesn't wake me up like that anymore.

The last time I went to Boston with Dad and Louis, I kept this diary, so that I could remember all the good and bad things.

Monday August 18th 2014

So we arrived late last night. We didn't even get to fly first class. How rude.

It was the first day at the hospital. We didn't have to be there till 9 a.m. but we were up at 6 a.m. anyway. The first thing I had was something called nursing intake which is basically a check-up. Then we did consent which is where the parents have to sign loads of forms and things that I don't really understand. Then I had to sit on a chair for five minutes and not talk or move, so the nurses can check my blood pressure. It's a lot harder than it seems. We saw Leslie as well, which was really nice as we haven't seen her in ages. I gave her a big hug, I think she needed it. It was kinda nice to see the doctors as well, given the circumstances. They are all lovely people.

Tuesday August 19th 2014

I couldn't eat breakfast today because I had a blood draw first thing. How fun! It was a good thing it only took forty minutes. As soon as I finished I went and had breakfast. I was feeling a bit weak and wobbly. On the way to breakfast we walked past Lindsay's room. She was there with her parents; they are such lovely family. Then we all sat down and had a meeting with Dr Leslie. From what I understood everything is going great. A lot of what Dr Leslie said went over my head, but mainly she told us the FTI drugs are working and everyone taking it is living longer, which is good. They're not sure if the statins and bisphonsphonate we were taking in the second and third round of trials have made much of a difference, so they are going to look into that a bit more. But my blood vessels are not so stiff, so there's less chance of me getting heart disease or having a stroke, which is nice to know.

After that we had to go through the drug log with the doctors. Dad had spent three hours filling it in the night before. The last test of the day was the ECG or Echocardiogram, which wasn't too bad. I had to take my top off and lie on the bed and the doctor put this really cold jelly on my chest. Then they put this probe thing, which looks like a really fat pen, on top of the jelly and moved it around so they could see my heart on the computer. They could see if the muscles in my heart are getting thicker, which would be a bad thing. But from what I could tell it's all looking good.

Wednesday August 20th 2014

Today we started at 10 a.m. with physical therapy. That was a quick visit because I can't do much physical therapy now that I don't walk. They bent my fingers right back to measure how far my joints would bend. They used to put building blocks on the floor one metre apart and I had to walk around them for six minutes, then they would take my blood pressure, but I don't have to do that anymore. They measured my elbows and knees and I had to stand up to find out how tall I was: 111cm. Last time I was 119cm. Dad said, 'it must be true that you shrink with age.' Not helpful. Then they put a thing against my leg and I had to push forward as hard as I could to see how strong I was. I don't think I was very strong.

After the physical tests we went for X-rays. I had to stand up to have my full body X-rayed. I thought I couldn't stand up. But the doctor helped me. Once I was standing up I was OK holding on to the machine, but I couldn't really move.

'Look at Hayley standing up,' Dad shouted.

I thought, 'Shut up.'

I can stand but I can't really move or walk very far unless there's something to hold on to. After that I had to lie down on my back for the DXA scan that measures how strong my bones are.

They have saved the 'best' for last today. MRI scan. Great! It's like the worst thing ever. I would rather have needles than go through that. I wish I didn't have to do it, but there's nothing I can do. I have to suck it up and be a man and get on with it. The machine looks like a massive doughnut-shaped tunnel from the outside. But inside it's really dark and claustrophobic. That's what I hate most, being in such a small space.

The first time I went into the scanner, the doctors said, 'It will probably sound like it's broken but it's not. Just lie still.'

I didn't have much choice as there's a massive thing on my chest that was holding me down. When the machine starts up it makes a loud banging and clicking sound, as if someone is trying to get in. It's so noisy I have to wear earplugs and headphones. I have to lie still for more than an hour, while it photographs my body. My feet stick out of the end and someone, usually Mum or Dad, holds on to my feet.

'If you need to stop, just wiggle your feet,' the doctors say.

Usually I try and take my mind off what's happening by singing songs in my head, but that doesn't always work because I want to start tapping my feet. This time it was so much better than usual. They gave me these special goggles and headphones so I could watch a film. And it was my favourite film, *Surf's Up*, so I got to watch Cody the surfing penguin while the machine did its thing. The hour went really quickly and I had to get out before the film ended. For the first time ever, I can say I quite enjoyed it. I wish they had invented those goggles years ago.

Thursday August 21st 2014

I couldn't eat breakfast again today because I had to have vascular assessments. They took my pulse and stuff and measured how fast my blood is going through my veins. It's the easy bit.

Before they let us go home on the night flight, we had to go and pick up the drugs for the next trial.

In between all the hospital stuff we had time to look around. Boston in August was so hot, like eighty degrees hot. But it was a nice hot, not that humid kind that makes you sweat. It made a change because normally we go in the middle of winter when it's snowing. I actually took my jumper off and wore a T-shirt, that's how hot it was.

Dad took me and Louis to Fenway Park, where the Boston Red Sox baseball team plays. We couldn't actually buy tickets to go inside and watch them play but we watched all the fans going in. The atmosphere was crazy. We also went to the Boston Beer Works near the Red Sox stadium and, surprise surprise, I ordered mash and gravy. The waitress put this massive plate in front of me and I took one look and thought 'gross'. The gravy was really pale and looked like dishwater. I wasn't holding out much hope. But I tried it and was like, 'Wow. This is so nice.' The mash was really creamy and the gravy was so tasty, even better than the red wine gravy Mum used to buy in a packet from Tesco. I had a massive plate full and I kept on eating and eating. I ate so much and I still had more left but I couldn't eat it all. It was the best mash ever - like ever. I can't wait to go back to Boston next time, just for the gravy.

On the journey home, a really embarrassing thing happened at the airport. We were going through check-in and put all our stuff through the scanner. Dad decides to shout out, 'I've got a bag of drugs here.'

Honestly! I didn't know where to look. Everyone was looking at us and Dad didn't seem at all bothered. He opened Louis' backpack, which was stuffed full of a two-year supply of my FTI drugs, and just went, 'See.' Luckily we had all the paperwork to go with it and they let us take it through. Dad thought it was really funny. But he wasn't laughing when we got back home and realised we'd left my iPad at the airport, so he had to buy me a new one.

Chapter 16

'Big Burps and Furry Arteries'

My health checks

The good thing about having progeria is that if ever I entered a burping competition I would most likely win. I know that sounds really weird, but the drugs I take give me this superhuman capacity to belch for Britain. My dad calls it 'my FTI burp'. It doesn't happen very often. But when it does, pass me a bucket and get out of my way!

I can't help it, blame the drugs. It first happened after the very first time I took the FTI tablets in 2007. We were walking through a shopping centre in Boston and I did this enormous burp, it was so embarrassing. Everyone turned around and stared at me. By the time we flew back home to Britain I felt really sick. I didn't want to eat anything; I just lay in bed, throwing up. Mum and Dad were really worried. I think they were frightened because they thought they were giving me tablets to make me better and they were actually making me worse. They thought the FTI drugs were having really bad side effects and I was going to die. I was a little bit scared, too.

In a panic, they rang the doctors in Boston who prescribed a drug called Zofran, which is used for people on chemotherapy to stop them being sick. It was a horrible time and it was weeks and weeks before I finally stopped being ill and got my appetite back.

Now I take a Zofran tablet every morning after my FTI and all is good. Except on the days when I forget to take it; then the FTI tells my stomach to empty itself ... so stand well back. It just comes without a warning. One minute I can be eating, then I start feeling a bit shaky, then I go quiet before unleashing a ground-shaking burp, followed by projectile vomit. Disgusting, I know, and it mostly happens when I'm staying with my dad, which is quite fortunate as Mum doesn't deal with sick so well. Dad says, 'When you've had six kids, you get used to sick,' and always keeps a bucket nearby.

The last time it happened we were having curry for supper. Within minutes I was tucking into my poppadoms again as if nothing had happened. Now I know what it is, it doesn't scare me; it's just one of those things. If Louis is in the same room, he gets into a flap and runs to fetch the bucket, but really it's more of an inconvenience than anything to panic about.

Because of my progeria, and the drug trials, I have to take a load of drugs every day. I keep them in a little red zipper wash bag that the airline gave us when we flew first class to Boston years ago. It's a bit worn now because it gets so much use. Every morning after my breakfast I take two FTIs and half a Zofran; half an Imodium as diarrhoea is another side effect of the FTI; a capsule of folic acid to stop me getting anaemic; and an Atenolol beta-blocker to prevent my blood pressure from getting dangerously high. Most of the tablets I take are the sort of things doctors give to old people. I also have to take a contraceptive pill, which I don't like talking about as I get embarrassed. Doctors told Mum that I wouldn't go through puberty but, just my luck, I have so I take the pill to stop my periods. I find it's too much effort to take all my meds in the morning, so before I go to bed at night I take another two FTIs and half an aspirin, which helps to stop my blood from clotting, and a statin to help lower the cholesterol in my blood.

The statins are prescribed by my cardiologist, Dr Graham Whincup, who is based at my local Conquest Hospital in Hastings. He says medicine is all about 'looking for the surprise and making sure it isn't a big surprise', so every three to six months Mum and I go to see him and he checks out my heart. We always go to see him and give him my medical records when we come back from Boston. Once we had to give him a CD with all the X-rays I have ever had taken in America, more than 3,000 of them. 'That's your bedtime reading,' Mum said and he laughed, nervously I thought.

Dr Whincup is the best doctor ever. He's really nice and friendly and always honest. He explains things in a way that's easy to understand. At one of our first appointments I remember he drew a picture of my heart on a piece of paper. It looked more like a circle than a heart shape. He drew lines for the chambers, blood vessels and valves and other bits and bobs like plaque and sticky bits and explained how he was going to keep checking for plaque that might build up inside the tubes carrying blood to my heart (arteries). High cholesterol can be dangerous for everyone as it leads to a hardening and narrowing of the arteries, or atherosclerosis to use its posh, proper medical name. When this happens it can be really serious as the arteries get all clogged up with fatty stuff and the blood can't flow properly. If one of those fatty things bursts it can cause a blood clot and lead to the person having a heart attack or a stroke, which have killed some of my friends. These days when we go to see Dr Whincup he does an Echocardiogram and shows us the inside of my heart on a monitor. That way he can check that my valves are not leaking, my arteries are not getting furry and the muscles in my heart are doing a good job of pumping the blood around my body.

I think Dr Whincup was a bit worried when I got an annoying cough. Sometimes coughs can be a sign of heart failure, but they can also be lots of other less sinister things. So he checked out my heart and was happy that wasn't the reason I'm coughing, which is a relief. Dr Whincup says I know far more about the heart than most of the medical students that he sometimes has sitting in with him. When I was younger I used to ask lots of questions because I was curious about what happened inside my body. But lately I don't ask too many questions, it's best not to know too much, I think. Although Dr Whincup is always honest and I know that if he wasn't happy with what he saw, he would tell us. But so far he says I'm amazing.

'Your heart is in better condition than mine', he always tells me.

I used to think that was a good thing, until Dad told me he has a pacemaker, so now I'm not so sure!

At the end of every appointment, as we are walking out the door, he says, 'No more roll-up Woodbines and give up alcohol.'

He knows that makes me smile and he likes to make me happy.

Dr Whincup always tells Mum that if any of the other families need advice about progeria he will help them, which is really nice. One mother wrote him a letter and called him the European Progeria Specialist. I think he was quite proud of that and a little bit embarrassed. The thing is he is like a specialist because progeria is so rare and he's been treating me for so long, so he knows more about it than most doctors. When he was a junior doctor working in Sheffield years and years ago he saw a couple of kids with progeria. Then my friend Maddie was cared for by another doctor at the Conquest Hospital and he sometimes helped her, so he really has had more experience than many doctors.

Lately I've been a bit worried about Dr Whincup, ever since his bosses banned him from wearing bow ties. For as long as I can remember he's always worn a bow tie. That's his thing. He's quite the gentleman, you see. Once when we were in Boston I saw a nice bow tie that I thought he would like, so I bought it for him as a thank you present. He used to wear it whenever I saw him. But the Health Trust which runs the hospital banned all ties because of health and safety issues. Really? I mean I know some doctors who wear normal ties have to be careful because little kids could grab them and pull them and they might choke or something. But if Dr Whincup had touched a patient with his bow tie, he would have been struck off years ago. He is trying to persuade them to lift the ban, so I hope next time I see him he'll be back to his old, bow-tie wearing and jolly self.

The thing that makes Dr Whincup the saddest is that he and all the other doctors couldn't provide me with a new pair of hips. When I was a little girl he would shout 'Hayley' as soon as he saw me, and I would run to him and he would pick me up and whirl me around his head. That always made me laugh. He can't do that now I'm in a wheelchair. I think he misses that, so I always make sure to give him big hugs. He has no reason to be sad; it's just one of those things.

Chapter 17

'I Want to Be the First Person With Progeria to Work in the Media'

Starting college

One of my favourite things to do is people-watching, and one of the best places for it is the cafeteria at Bexhill Sixth Form College. Boys with tattooed necks and piercings all over their faces; girls with green, blue and pink hair. I love it. On my first day at college I remember just sitting with my new teaching assistant, Lana Castle, looking at people with all their weird hair styles. I was actually quite surprised to see so many people wearing all sorts of hip clothes and brightly coloured hair. It made a change after high school, where even a pocket on your trousers was banned. I have decided that if I had hair I would definitely want to dye it a different colour every week, probably green or blue. It would probably fall out because of all of the dye.

My first taste of college life was at an open day, back in the summer of 2014 when all of the students were on holiday, so it seemed quiet. When I was offered a place, I was really excited. I would be starting all over again with a new place, new people and the chance to meet a whole set of new friends. The last night of the summer holidays I went to bed thinking, 'Yay! College tomorrow.' But when my alarm went off the next morning, my stomach was doing back flips, I was so nervous.

But once I got there and met my new TA, Lana, I felt 'You can do this.' At first I was sad that my old TA, Mrs G, couldn't leave high school and come with me to college. I even threatened to get her the sack, so she would have no choice but to come with me, but that didn't happen. Lana is only twenty-three. She is blonde and friendly and we get along just fine, she has similar taste in music and we have lots to talk about. The good thing about college is that people are there because they want to learn, not because they have to be there. Everyone seems so much older and more mature, so it's a totally different atmosphere.

Bexhill College is massive, they have 1,500 students, but only two others are in wheelchairs. They have hundreds of courses in science, photography, media, travel and tourism, hairdressing, child care, dance and performing arts. It has science laboratories, music and recording studios, dance and film studios. It even has its own theatre, the Izzard Theatre, named after Bexhill's most famous person, the comedian Eddie Izzard. He actually opened it and apparently he said it was bonkers to name a theatre after him.

My course is Level 2 Media Studies. It only takes a year and is equivalent to a GCSE. My course tutors – Becky Crouch, who is the deputy head of the creative arts department, and another tutor, Lindsey Parker – are both really nice and helpful. The media suite, where I have most of my lessons, is on the second floor. There are thirteen other students on my course, but only three girls. In the first few days I recognised quite a few people from school and from around Bexhill. My desk is at the front of the class, so I am able to hear the tutor. Sitting next to me is a girl called Rachel, who used to be in my class in school.

Most of the course is practical and based on coursework, so there are no exams at the end of the year. Bonus! I'm going to be learning loads about the advertising industry, looking at how adverts are designed for magazines, radio and TV and how we remember them. I'll also be designing advertisements and film posters using Photoshop, which will be really cool as I like playing around with photos. I'll also be studying animation, making a music video, which will be good fun, and learning about print production and how posters and magazines are made. I already know a little bit about printing, as Mum and I went to a printing press in Croydon to see my last book, *Old Before My Time*, come off the printing press. It was so strange seeing thousands of copies of my face whizzing around a factory.

For my first college assignment I had to write a diary of all the media we use. That was easy, Twitter, Twitter, music and a bit of TV. For another assignment I had to study three UK music magazines, *NME*, *We Love Pop* and *Kerrang!*, and look at the age of their readers and the kind of music they like. Now I'm really into *Kerrang!*, which is a rock music magazine. The good thing about college is that after you hand in an assignment you get ten days to improve it for a better grade. Some people have started to get stressed by the amount of assignments we have to hand in, but I'm good with my work and make sure I leave myself plenty of time to do it properly.

My timetable also has three maths lessons a week, which is bad news, but I'm not the only one. There are hundreds of people who have to resit maths, so I don't feel so bad knowing I'm not the only person who is rubbish at it. I have quite a few free periods during the week, when I can catch up on homework or people-watching. Some days I don't have to start until 11.30, which is good. Wednesdays is enrichment day. It sounds quite posh, but it's just another word for extra-curricular clubs. There were loads of different things to choose: rowing, football, photography and quidditch. I have chosen music, so I hope we will get the chance to learn to play an instrument. I really want to learn to play the guitar like Luke from 5SOS but it might be too difficult to hold down the strings with my little fingers. I will have to get one with nylon strings. When I was in primary school I learnt to play the violin. I can't really remember much, but Mum tells me she was pregnant with Ruby at the time, so I must have been seven or eight. I used to sit next to Mum and play 'Twinkle, Twinkle Little Star'. Mum would laugh and tell me, 'That's beautiful, Hayley' and I used to say 'Aren't I clever?' All the time Ruby would be kicking inside Mum's stomach, I think she was probably trying to get away from the noise.

If I work really hard at college, I will be able to move up to Level 3 next year which will be like an A Level and after that, who knows, I could even go to university, but I think that would be too scary. I really want to be a journalist. I'm a big fan of teen magazines like *Top of the Pops* magazine and *Bliss*, even though they've stopped printing. I love reading interviews with famous people and I would like to find out more about the people they interview and see what they are like in real life.

I've always thought it would be great to go to work, interview the latest bands, and get paid. Once I wrote to *Bliss* asking if I could do work experience, they told me to send them a CV, so I did. I showed off a bit and said I had been on TV and in magazines, but I didn't get a reply. How rude. A few months later I found it had closed down, so that might explain why. I don't know of any other people with progeria who work in the media, so I would like to be the first.

Chapter 18

'Music, Music and More Music'

My favourite bands

It's so hard to imagine a world where there would be no music. I can't even think about it without getting upset. Music and bands are my life. I know that makes me sound like such a fan girl. You might think that sounds weird but it's acceptable because I'm a teenager and we're allowed to be a bit obsessive. I will probably grow out of it one day but for now, it's fun.

My mum was the same when she was a teenager. She used to love Madonna and bought all her albums. When she told me, I thought, 'Wow, now we understand each other.' Mum has terrible taste in music, she likes dance music, all that stuff made with computers and keyboards, and I like bands that play actual instruments like guitars and drums.

For as long as I can remember I've always been a bit obsessed with pop stars. In our photo album there's a picture of me when I was about eight being hugged by Kylie Minogue. It was taken when I met her at one of the rehearsals for her *Showgirl* tour in 2004. I'm wearing a pink beaded bandana and a big grin and Kylie is holding me up in one arm and punching the air with the other.

When I was thirteen I used to be mad about Justin Bieber and wanted to meet him. My friends and followers started a #BiebsmeetHayley campaign on Twitter. It spread around the world and got back to his manager, who called Mum to arrange a secret meeting in London. There I was thinking that we were going shopping and I ended up in this really posh hotel with Justin Bieber. When I first saw him, I screamed and ran to hug him but my arms only came as far as his waist. Mum took a photo of us together, me with Justin Bieber holding me in his arms. I kept thinking, 'I am the luckiest girl in the world. Justin Bieber is hugging me!' I met him again a couple of months later when I went to his concert and got invited backstage by Willow Smith, who was supporting him on tour. I don't know if all the stories about him getting arrested, throwing eggs, taking drugs and being drunk are true. But I think he needs to sort himself out and if I ever get to meet him again, I will tell him.

My new favourite bands are The Wanted, even though they are not together any more, and The Vamps and 5SOS, and the punk band Green Day. I met The Wanted before I was even a fan. Mum's friend was taking her daughter to see them in Brighton so Mum bought tickets for us to go too. *Old Before My Time* had just been published, so Mum said we should take a copy and give it to them as a present. We arrived at the Brighton Centre really early to pick up our tickets. The woman working in the box office saw us and said 'Haven't I seen you on TV?' Mum said yes and the woman said she was so pleased to meet me. Then she let us sneak into the main hall where The Wanted were sound-checking. I walked in and had no idea who they were; I didn't even know their names. But they were so nice and friendly. On the way out I thought I would give the box office lady the copy of the book I had in my bag, because she had been so nice to us. She was so thrilled, she started to cry, which was a bit awkward, then asked if I would sign it.

'Thank you,' she said.

'No, thank you,' I said. 'Because you let me meet the band.'

I can still remember the day when I got my first tweet from The Wanted. I was in the back of the car and Mum was driving us to our first UK Progeria Reunion in Kent when I saw something on Twitter called 'Fan Friday'. It was a thing where members of the band asked a question and they would follow the fan that came up with the funniest answer. I remember the exact tweet. The question they put out was 'If Nathan (i.e. my favourite band member Nathan Sykes) was at the airport, what three things would he buy in the duty-free shop?' So I tweeted, 'He wouldn't buy anything because he would be at the lost children's meeting place.' OK, so it might not make sense to you but there was a story behind it. Every Wednesday was 'Wanted Wednesday', where they would send an email out to fans telling them what they'd been doing throughout the week and a link to a video. I would sit for hours and

MY PHOTO GALLERY

This section is some of my own photographs mostly taken along the coast and countryside near my home in Sussex plus a few of my favourite photos from the family album.

hours watching every single 'Wanted Wednesday' video, reading all the tweets. It was such fun. In one of these videos the band was in a park, looking for Nathan, who is the youngest member. They couldn't find him anywhere. Then they saw him standing on his own at the lost children's meeting place. I thought I was being so creative and funny with my tweet. So when they replied, 'Yeah you're right', I was so happy and excited that my first contact with the band was making fun of Nathan.

The second time I met the band in person was a year later at the Brighton Centre again. By that time Ruby had started playing their songs, like 'Glad You Came', 'Lightning' and 'All Time Low', so they just rubbed off on me and I really liked them. I knew who they were, I knew all their names and through my connections with them on Twitter I knew all about each band member. I knew that Tom Parker was the oldest and I admired him because he didn't care what people thought about him. I knew that Max George looked all stern and intimidating but was really happy and one of the nicest people ever. I knew that Jay McGuinness, the one with the curly hair, was always telling jokes and making everyone laugh. I knew Siva Kaneswaran was cuddly and warm and gave the best hugs. I also knew that Nathan Sykes was my favourite. When I say favourite, I like him only a little bit more than the others. In every band there is someone you connect with most and for me it's Nathan because he is genuine and sweet and doesn't judge people on their actions or appearances. I think it's OK to have a favourite in a band but it's not OK to have a least favourite. A lot of girls like Nathan the best because he is the youngest, but that's not why I like him. I just think he's nice and he said he would try and take me to the prom, even though he didn't in the end.

The next time I saw The Wanted they were performing a special concert at the Shepherd's Bush Empire in London and I was lucky to get a ticket. It was an intimate show with only five hundred fans. Mum took me and Courtney to the concert. She dropped us off at the venue and we waited to go in and meet them.

When we walked in they were rehearsing and they stopped and said, 'Look, it's Hayley.'

I thought, 'I can't believe that they remembered me after a year.' It was the best thing ever just to hear them say my name.

As Jay walked past me he said, 'You all right, trouble?'

Then Max came up and said, 'Me so horny', and beeped the horn on my wheelchair; that made me laugh.

Later when Mum picked us up after the concert, she said, 'That Tom is nice.'

I said, 'Yeah, I know he's nice. '

I thought it was a bit of a random thing to say until she said, 'I was outside having a fag with him.'

Turns out that my Mum was waiting around the back door, smoking, and Tom popped out for a sneaky fag and asked my mum for a light. How cool is that, my mum actually had a fag with one of The Wanted? After that Mum liked them as well, but her favourite is Max. Mum reckons that The Wanted are the one the reason I cheered up after my hip problems. I do really like them all and they are all so easy to talk to. I've met them loads of times. That's another perk of having progeria – and a 'friend' working at the Brighton Centre. Not only do I get the best view at the side of the stage in a special area for wheelchairs, but I also get to go backstage to meet bands. Normally fans have to pay for a meet and greet, but I don't. A lot people dislike me for that and think it's really out of order. But it's OK as I'm special and I don't make the rules.

I have a special necklace that Nathan once gave me backstage at one of their concerts. I just happened to mention that I liked his necklace.

'Thanks,' he said and we carried on talking a bit more.

Then, just as I was leaving he turned round and said, 'Hey girlfriend, you want this necklace?'

'OK,' I said. So he took it off and put it around my neck.

Later he tweeted, 'With my favourite person in the world, @Hayleyokinesx. Love this girl! Everyone follow.'

How sweet is that? I want to marry him. I've met his sister and everything; we are friends on Twitter.

Every time I meet my favourite band, I think it's polite to buy them a present. Once I adopted a shark as a present for Max because I know he likes sharks. I've given Tom a silver guitar pick with his name engraved because he plays guitar and I've made them scrapbooks, where I've spent weeks collecting funny photos I've taken of them or cutting pictures out of magazines. I like to leave them with something and hope they will remember me.

As I've already told you, Courtney's favourite band is Lawson. When she saw on Facebook that they were going to be in Brighton, signing copies of their new record, she asked me if I wanted to go. Now I'm not a massive fan like Courtney and Brighton was a long way, so I told her I wasn't bothered. When the day arrived Courtney still really wanted to go and all day in school she kept asking me to go with her. So in the middle of a lesson I texted Mum and said, 'Mum, you know you love me. So can I go to Brighton tonight with Courtney?'

She said 'What?'

'I told you about it the night before,' I said.

She replied, 'But you said you didn't want to go.'

'Well, now I do, so can I?'

She couldn't really say no because she's always going on that I should get out more. So she picked me up from school and we rushed down to the station to catch the train to Brighton.

It was the first time I'd been out to Brighton without Mum and I was quite scared, so I texted her every couple of minutes.

'We're on the train.'

'We're almost there.'

'We're there.'

'Just got off the train.'

'We're in KFC.'

'On our way to HMV now.'

'What if one of the band knows you?' Courtney said as we were on our way to the shop.

'Don't be stupid,' I replied. 'Why would they know me?'

I guess she's so used to complete strangers coming up to me and recognising me from TV.

When we got to the shop hundreds of fans were already waiting in line. A photographer from the evening newspaper was there taking photos of all the fans as they queued up and sang Lawson songs. Courtney and I joined the end of the line. Just as I was thinking that we would have to wait ages to get to see the band, one of the progeria perks happened. The lead singer walked past and said, 'Hello, Hayley. Haven't I seen you on TV?'

I said, 'Goodness me.'

'See, I told you,' Courtney said.

She was almost crying with happiness, so much that I thought she was going to pass out.

'Shut up,' I said, and we followed him to the front of the queue, where the band signed a copy of their new CD for us. Then the photographer from the newspaper asked us to smile and took our photograph with the band. The following day it was in the paper and Courtney's friends were a bit jealous. I was really glad I decided to go with her and came away loving Lawson.

Did you know that the reason they are called Lawson is because their lead singer Andy Brown had a brain tumour and his doctor was called Dr David Lawson so they named the band after the man who saved his life. If I had a band I would have to call it Whincup after my doctor.

I would spend all my pocket money going to concerts if I could. I won tickets to see The Vamps playing a charity concert for the Teenage Cancer Trust. All I had to do was text £5 and I won. How lucky was that? We also had tickets to a Rays of Sunshine Concert at the Royal Albert Hall, which was really cool. It's like a charity that grants wishes for kids like me and they give free tickets, so Mum got tickets to take me and Courtney.

My next goal in life is to meet the band 5SOS. Mum has bought me tickets to go and see them twice next year. I gave Mum a very convincing argument why I needed to see them, which basically came down to:

A. They are one of my favourite bands

B. I've never seen them live in person

C. Mum says I should get out and meet more friends

D. I have arranged to meet up with my Twitter friend Shannon.

I'm so in love with Ashton, their drummer, that I think if I do ever get to meet them I'm actually scared that I will hug him and I won't be able to let go. I'm kind of nervous that his arms would probably crush me.

Happy days!

Chapter 19

'I'd Much Rather Be Behind the Camera'

Why I like taking photos but hate being photographed

I like taking photographs, like my dad. He says I'm a pretty good photographer. Sometimes he takes me down to the beach or parks and places where I can snap away. For Christmas Dad got me a Canon Coolpix, a really cool camera. I don't know all the technical terms for it but it's red and I love it. The best thing is that it's light enough for me to hold and has a viewfinder that I can look through to see what I'm taking a photo of. I hate those digital cameras that just have a screen; it's not like proper photography. I used to borrow my dad's camera, which was a really good, but I couldn't hold it for long because it was so heavy. Dad says you take better photographs with a heavy camera – at least that's what some photographers have told him. My camera has got a zoom lens, so I can get in really close to things. I can be on the seafront at Bexhill taking a photo of something half a mile away in really close detail. If I was a private investigator, it would be really good to spy on people.

I like taking close-up photos of plants and flowers, butterflies and beaches, surfs and sunsets, and even my fingernails.

'You know how to pick a good shot,' Dad says when we go out taking photos.

Once we were on a day trip to a butterfly farm and I wanted to take a picture of a bright blue butterfly sitting on a leaf. The contrast between the green and the blue looked really good. As I was taking my picture the butterfly fell off the leaf and dropped to the floor and died. I didn't know what to do. I thought I had killed it. So I covered it with grass and held a little funeral for it. Then I found out that most butterflies only live for like a week or two. It must be so sad to have a life so short.

I'm always messing about with photos on my iPhone and uploading them to Instagram. I have loads of different apps. One lets me turn the pictures into black and white and add colour in an area; another lets me write on them, which is really useful when I want to put funny photos on Twitter. Some have loads of special effects and different fonts, so it looks like I've written on the photo by hand and others put borders on the pictures. When I did my GSCE art project, Order and Disorder, Mum put some of the photos I took for it on Facebook and people were asking where they could buy them, which was really strange as they were just photos of traffic cones and drains or lines on the road. Some people have said I should think about selling my photographs and artwork, which I might do one day.

It's weird because although I have spent most of my life in front of the camera, I would much rather be behind it. Because progeria is so rare, the media are fascinated by me and I'm always being asked to appear on TV programmes, do interviews for newspapers and magazines and go to special awards. It all started when I was four and a documentary company from Channel 5's *Extraordinary People* series followed our family for a year to make the programme 'The Girl Who Is Older Than Her Mother'. That was followed by 'The Girl Who Is Older Than her Grandmother', 'The 96-Year-Old Schoolgirl' and 'The World's Oldest Teenager'. I hate being called old, because I don't feel any different from other teenagers, but millions of people all over the world still watch them.

When I turned fourteen I stopped making TV documentaries, I just got sick of having the cameras following me around everywhere. Enough people stare at me anyway and when you walk around with a camera even more people stare. So I decided I'd had enough, someone else can have a turn.

I'm not sorry that I made so many documentaries because they've been shown all over the world and it has helped other families to know more about progeria. One little girl called Lucy, who lives in Ireland and is only four, got in touch with Mum because she'd seen one of my programmes and there's a family in Japan that have been in touch with the Progeria Research Foundation because they saw me doing the drug trials, so it's not all bad.

Through the media I have met loads of famous people and had some amazing experiences, most of which you'll already know about if you've read my first book *Old Before My Time*. I used to attend the Children of Courage Awards held by *Woman* magazine every year, where I met everyone from HRH Prince Charles to pop princess Kylie Minogue. Film crews from Australia's *60 Minutes* TV programme have flown to Britain to talk to me; I've been interviewed by one of America's most famous presenters, Barbara Walters, on the ABC news channel's programme *The View*, and back home in the UK I've been featured on BBC *Breakfast* and *The Jeremy Kyle Show*.

It's just that the older I get, the stroppier I'm getting. I hate it when someone is talking to you and there's an awkward silence and I have no idea what to say or do. On TV it's usually OK because the presenters know they can't have awkward silences on screen, so they know what to say. And anyway Mum or Dad is usually with me and they do most of the talking while I just sit there. For example, the last time we went to Boston Dad and I were asked to go into the Fox News 25 Studios to be interviewed about the drug trials and the Annual International Race For Research, which the Progeria Research Foundation run every year to raise money for the drug trials. Dad and Dr Leslie's sister Audrey Gordon did most of the talking and I just sat there looking awkward. I always I watch myself after the interview and think, 'OMG! Why did I say that?' or 'I should have said this.'

Another time when we were in Boston Mum asked if I would mind being filmed for some TV programme. I said, 'That's a stupid question, I don't think so.'

It's bad enough having needles and all that poking and prodding without having a camera in my face. No, thank you. I'm not comfortable when random people come up to me in the street and say 'Haven't I seen you on TV?' It happens a lot when I'm out with my friend Courtney. I know they are just being friendly but I don't know what to say. I can see it's awkward for Courtney and it's awkward for me because I'm with my friends.

I know what you're thinking. If you hate being in front of the camera so much, how did you have your photograph taken for the cover of this book? Well, that was a bit different because the photographer Jason Fry is a good photographer and I know him like a friend because he's taken loads of pictures for the Progeria Reunions and has helped me with tips for taking my own photos. With some photographers they take ages getting the lighting just right and then they want you to smile a million different ways and I just get so bored. But Jason knows how to make me feel relaxed and gets good shots straight away.

In 2012 I was nominated for an award in the Argus Achievement Awards. The awards were being held at the Theatre Royal in Brighton. Mum was nominated for Mum of the Year and I was up for Courageous Child of the Year. Mum of the Year went to a woman whose nine-year-old son had asthma and had an anaphylactic attack and actually died. I was a bit disappointed for Mum.

When they started calling out the names for my award, I got butterflies in my stomach as I had to go up to the stage to get the award. There were a couple of other kids who went up first. One boy was only five and had a rare muscle-wasting disease; another boy was thirteen and had brittle bone disease and did a sponsored walk for Great Ormond Street Hospital, one boy had saved his friend from drowning in the sea, a two-year-old girl had a really rare condition that made her have seizures and one boy had beaten cancer twice but wasn't there because he had fallen ill again. When they called my name, it wasn't too bad. I went to the stage and everyone was looking at me and clapping, which was just a bit embarrassing, but I got £100, which was very nice.

Chapter 20

My Life in a Day

People often ask me what it's like living with progeria as if I must have some really exciting or unusual life. But the reality is, I'm no different from any other teenager. I still have to get up, go to college and do all the regular, boring stuff. So here, in a nutshell, is a diary of my typical day. So you can believe me when I say it's not that exciting.

7.15 a.m.: My phone alarm wakes me up with music by my favourite band, currently 5 Seconds of Summer. It's just so I can wake up and get used to the world around me. I don't understand 'morning people' like Ruby and my mum. They can jump out of bed as soon as their alarms go off. I can't do that *ever*. I have to lie in the dark for at least ten minutes, slowly regaining consciousness. I lie there listening to my favourite songs, trying to get my eyes to open while the rest of my family comes to life. I love my bedroom: it is cosy and has black and silver swirly patterned wallpaper on the walls and matching curtains, which I chose. Not that you can see much of the wallpaper as I have so many posters of my favourite bands pinned to the walls along with my laminated The Wanted tour passes from the times I've been backstage at their concerts.

7.30 a.m.: My alarm goes off again. This time Jesus of Suburbia by Green Day so I know it's time to get up. Mum, Ruby and Louis are already moving around. I sit up, swing my legs over the side of the bed and get into my wheelchair. Then I get the lift downstairs to the kitchen, banging the doors and knocking over radiator covers as I go. I'm in such a bad mood first thing in the morning, that Mum knows it's best not to talk to me for at least ten minutes, until I've had my cup of tea. Even at weekends, when I wake up naturally at 11.30 am, I'm still in a bad mood. I think I must get it from my mum. She says she can't talk to anyone unless she's had her first fag of the day.

7.40am: Mum will make me a cup of tea (weak and milky with at least two sugars, if you must know), while I get my breakfast ready. Mum always leaves my bowl and cereal out on the worktop for me because I can't reach the cupboards but I can get to the milk in the fridge. Before I eat my breakfast, I take my tablets. Then I go into the lounge and sit in front of the TV while I eat my breakfast from a special, low coffee table beside the sofa.

7.45 a.m.: Read Twitter. It's important I spend at least ten minutes catching up on the news and photos, while Mum reads the newspaper. Checking on all my bands makes the start of my day happy.

8.10 a.m.: Still eating breakfast. It can take me forty minutes to eat a bowl of Coco Pops, because I have to wait for them to go soggy before I can eat them.

8.15 a.m.: Relax and read some more tweets, while Mum runs around getting my clothes ready. I can put on my tops and hoodies myself, but Mum has to help me out with my trousers and shoes. She also has to tie my bandana in a knot at the back of my head. No one can fold and tie my bandana as well as my mum. I remember, when my friend Maddie was still alive, we would take our bandanas off in school and tie them under our chins to look like nuns. Our mothers used to despair.

8.20 a.m.: I casually wheel myself to the bathroom go to the toilet, wash my face, brush my teeth, wash my face, wipe the sleep out of my eyes, spray myself with Taylor Swift perfume, then I'm out of the door.

8.25 a.m.: Sit in the back of the car, listening to music on my headphones. One of the good things about being in college is that it's further away, so I get to hear a whole song in the car. When I was at school I could only listen to half a song.

8.30 a.m.: Arrive at college, meet my TA, go to our first lectures of the day. Depending on what day of the weeks it is, these can start at 9 am or 11.30 am. When I was in school, lessons always started at 9 am.

Mid-morning: Check Twitter for a couple of minutes during the break. I try not to spend too much time on my phone when I'm in college because it's rude to sit glued to the phone when my TA is with me. And it costs too much. Sometimes during the break, I'll meet with Courtney if her timetable allows or I'll go to the canteen with my TA.

11.30 a.m.: More lectures.

1 p.m.: Lunch. Check Twitter. Eat Oreos. Drink water.

4 p.m.: Mum or Dad will drive me home in the car. When I get home I'll have another cup of tea and a piece of toast. When I say toast, I mean warm bread spread with an inch of butter. I'll check Twitter to make sure nothing major has happened in the two hours since I last looked, while Mum cooks dinner.

5.30 p.m.: We'll have dinner. Normally I just have a bowl of potato: new potato; mashed potato; roast potato; or boiled potato with just butter or ketchup. Sometimes if Mum is cooking pasta, I'll have a bowl of pasta with no sauce, just butter. I eat so much butter I'm surprised I haven't had a heart attack. I love Yorkshire puddings; I like a roast dinner but I don't like meat. I can eat healthy food. I like carrots, cauliflower and broccoli, and roast dinners without meat or swede; I just choose not to eat them. Most nights it takes me about an hour to eat my dinner. Mum says it's because I have a little mouth – not. When the melted butter goes cold and hard and congealed, it's disgusting, so Mum has to reheat it in the microwave a couple of times. My very favourite food at the moment is poppadoms. I can eat a whole pack in one go, by accident. I don't mean to, they just seem to disappear.

6.30 p.m.: Once Mum has cleared away the dinner plates, we sit down to watch our favourite soap, *Hollyoaks*. I'm embarrassed to admit watching it, because it's so unrealistic. But I do and sometimes, if it's really exciting, we'll watch the next episode.

7 p.m.: I'll go up to my room and watch *The Vampire Diaries* on my iPad on Netflix. It's all about a teenager called Elena who falls in love with a really old vampire. When her brother Jeremy was killed by a bad vampire I cried, it was so sad. Sometimes I'll stay in the lounge and watch *Come Dine With Me* or *The Simpsons*, while my Mum will go upstairs and watch TV in her bedroom. She says 'You know you're getting old when you go to bed before your kids.' Ruby usually goes to bed at 8.30 p.m. and Louis at 9.30 p.m., but most nights he's still playing on his Xbox when I'm trying to go to sleep. Before I go to bed I always make sure take my pills.

10.30 p.m.: Turn off the lights and try to go to sleep. But I always end up texting or tweeting my friends on my phone. My logic is that if it's dark and I lie down, I will feel tired, but usually I am still awake at 11 p.m. On the weekends I'll still be on my phone at midnight. Sometimes I hear Mum snoring through the wall in her bedroom next door and I can't sleep. She says she doesn't snore, but I've recorded her a few times and played it back to her. It's worse in the summer because she leaves the door open and it sounds like a rhinoceros has got into her room. Once I accidentally went to sleep at 2 a.m. Mum asked, 'How can you accidentally stay awake till 2 a.m.?' But I was talking to my friend on Skype and didn't realise how late it was, honest.

Chapter 21

'Mum Says I'll Be Re-incarnated as a Sloth'

My dreams for the future

It's weird, but when I was younger I used to have this dream that one day I would leave home and move to New York and open a beauty salon. Now that I am actually old enough to leave home, I've changed my mind.

I would still like to get a place of my own, but I won't be able to move too far away from my mum. There is a new block of flats being built near where I live in Bexhill. It would be nice to move in there as I would still be close enough to Mum to be able to ring her up and ask her to pick me up a pint of milk or bar of chocolate and stuff. I'm not even sure if I could live by myself as I would be too scared. I have an overactive imagination as it is. Whenever I'm lying in bed and hear noises I always think there's someone in the house. So I would probably have to ask my friend Courtney, or Shannon, to move in with me.

I guess that if I plan to get my own flat, I'll need to get a job. I really want to be a journalist but most of the magazines I'd like to work for are based in London and London is such a massive place, I don't think I would be able to live there.

Now that I have turned seventeen I want to learn to drive. But I've no idea how it will work with me in the wheelchair. I can't even drive my wheelchair very well, so I'm not sure I'd be safe behind the wheel of a car. The problem is I get easily distracted. One minute I'll be looking at the road, and then I'll be looking at a nice cloud in the sky and crash into a wall or something. That would not be good. I can imagine being arrested and the police asking me, 'Why did you run over this person in your car?' 'Because I was listening to my favourite song on the radio' is not a defence.

I don't believe in marriage. That sounds really bad, but I don't think I'll ever get married; it's just a waste of money. My mum and dad were only married for four years before they got divorced. I read online that one in four marriages end in divorce. It's a lot of money and stress just to have your name on a bit of paper that says you're married. If you really love someone you don't need a bit of paper to tell you. I'm not really bothered about finding love; I'd rather have lots of cats and dogs.

I don't think that when you die that's the end to it. I think you become a ghost or get reincarnated. Mum is always telling me that one day I'm going to be reincarnated as a sloth, because I take so long doing things. I definitely believe in ghosts because I've had far too many spooky things happen to me. For example, on Christmas Day a couple of years ago, it was snowing and I got my first phone. I decided to play around with it and stood by the back door filming the snow in the garden. When I looked at the video there was a massive white light on the floor and nothing to explain it. I'm convinced it was a ghost.

Another time I was lying in bed watching TV on my iPad. Mum and Ruby were asleep and Louis was playing on his Xbox. All of a sudden he came into my room and said, 'Why did you call me?'

I told him I hadn't said anything and he said, 'I heard you call my name a couple of times.' That was really creepy.

I've heard voices too. Not long after my friend Maddie passed away, I was out shopping with my mum and I heard Maddie shouting my name. I haven't heard Maddie's voice for a long time, but the other night when I was lying in bed late at night I heard a child's voice talking out loud and it freaked me out. So I really do think there's something after life. I wouldn't complain if I came back as a sloth, there are far worse things to be.

⚡ Bucket List *

1) Go Stargazing

2) See all my favourite bands live

3) Finish College with a better than average grade

4) Get a munchkin cat (Probably name it Munchkin)

5) Have a bonfire on the beach with my friends

6) Meet Five Seconds of Summer, tell them they're idiots, hug them forever ☺

7) Hug a Sloth (a baby one)

8) Meet a turtle

9) Get matching tattoos with Shannon and Courtney

10) Go on a road trip with Shannon and Courtney

11) Go to Las vegas

12) Do a world wide reunion

13) Drive Route 66

14) Visit a ghost town

15) Go ghost hunting

A Mother's Story
by Kerry Okines

It's never easy being the mother of a teenager, but being the mother of a teenager with a limited lifespan is doubly difficult. Every morning when the rock music blares out from her bedroom and I hear her wheelchair moving around, I feel relief. It's as if every day we move further away from the dreaded age of thirteen is a bonus. When Hayley was younger it seemed as if I focused all my energy on organising surprises to make her life special and searching for answers to the important question, 'How can we cure progeria?' Now I ask myself 'What can I do to make her happy?'

I think back to some of the opportunities we've had as a family, the amazing places we've visited and the famous people we've met, and sometimes I have to pinch myself. The *Woman's Own* Children of Courage Awards where Hayley met HRH Prince Charles and broke all the rules asking him for a royal autograph; the visit to 10 Downing Street to meet the Prime Minister, Tony Blair; backstage with Cheryl Cole and Girls Aloud at one of their concerts; dress rehearsals with Kylie Minogue; posh hotels with Justin Bieber; presenting her own charity CD to Simon Cowell. The list goes on. Every famous person we met was smitten by Hayley's infectious personality. Then there were the months, that stretched into years, when we allowed the film cameras to follow our every move making Hayley's TV documentaries; these are all special opportunities that have come from being the parent of a child that is one in eight million. But I would trade them all for a future where Hayley and I could have the strong mother-daughter relationship that I have with my mum. It's only natural that teenagers don't want to hang out with their parents. Louis is about to hit that age and in a few years Ruby will also want more independence. But with Hayley I feel more and more redundant.

To the outside world I give the impression I'm tough and know how to play the shitty hand we've been dealt. But when we're alone, I go to a very dark place. The cloud of depression is always waiting to smother me. It started as a cry for help after Hayley was diagnosed with progeria. For months I harboured thoughts of killing myself, taking Hayley with me. But as the years passed, I learnt to cope and the happiness Hayley brought into our lives made me realise that having a child with such a rare disease was something to be celebrated, not a curse. But as time ticks on I have started to become more withdrawn. Whereas I could go for months without having black thoughts, some mornings I wake up and think, it's one day closer to the inevitable. I shut myself away from everyone and spend all my time watching TV or looking at Facebook. For so long I've been putting on a brave face, telling myself that everything is okay and I'm coping but it seems that the strain of holding everything together, has finally caught up with me. My doctor says it's my body's way of telling me it's had enough. Sometimes when the children are staying with their father I have been known to stay in bed all day, just watching daytime TV and sleeping. I feel as if my life is wasting away, I don't have anything to look forward to and have everything to dread. I am so negative all the time; when I used to be so full of energy.

At my darkest moments I call my mum and tell her, 'I've had enough.'

'Have a good cry, you'll feel better,' she says.

But I'm too scared. If I cry, I will never stop. I feel like I could just roll up into a ball and take my last breath. From the minute I wake up I have a feeling of dread that I can't suppress. I try to be positive, but inside I'm slowly dying. It's a time bomb, counting down closer to zero. I don't know how I get through some days; I just want to pack a bag and run away from everyone and everything, so I won't have to face the future.

People who have never suffered depression don't understand how oppressive the feelings can be. 'Just get out of bed, get dressed, and get out,' my sister tells me. If only it were that easy. My doctor prescribed me anti-depressant pills and referred me to a cognitive behavioural therapist, who told me that I needed to change the negative thoughts to positive. While she was explaining how the negative thoughts are caused by a chemical imbalance in the brain, all I could think was, 'Hayley is still going to have progeria and I'm still going to have these thoughts, so how can you make me change them?'

But I have to be open-minded and try and focus on the good things in my life, I have Louis and Ruby and I still have Hayley. I know that when I am down, my close friend Angela is only a phone call away in Scotland. Angela's daughter Claire was fourteen when she died of progeria. She is one of the very few mothers who can truly understand what I am feeling. She adored Claire just as much I love Hayley.

'I want to shake you, Kerry,' she says. 'You're grieving for Hayley when you should be enjoying your time together.'

I have so much to be grateful for. Hayley is still fit and healthy. Her heart is strong and her blood vessels are not as stiff as they used to be, all positive signs in keeping her risk of a heart attack or stroke low. It's a sign that our decision to allow her to be a guinea pig in the Progeria Research Foundation's clinical trials in Boston, all those years ago, seems to be paying off.

So much more is known now about the disease than back in the late 1990s when we first heard about it. Through the work of our friends Dr Leslie Gordon and her husband Dr Scott Berns at the PRF, the number of known cases of children living with Hutchinson-Gilford progeria has also gone up from forty to ninety-one and more than half of those children are now getting treatment.

The network of families is growing too. When Hayley was first diagnosed back in 1999, we didn't have a computer, let alone a window to a world where all families could be friends on Facebook. Over the years more and more children in all corners of the world have been identified, among them the first ever black child, a young girl living in South Africa. Some, like four-year-old Lucy who lives in Ireland, have tracked us down through Hayley's TV documentaries, which are still shown all over the world.

Our dream of a cure is still a long way off. But every day I pray they will hurry up and find that breakthrough before time runs out for our family. So far the results coming from Boston have been encouraging. Hayley and the twenty-seven other children who started taking the FTI drug Lonafarnib in 2007 have lived an average of 1.6 years longer, and we hope that will keep going up as the research continues. Only five of out of forty-three children on the drugs have passed away compared to twenty-one who were not taking the drugs. For our family I know it's been more than we could ever have wished for. The fact that Hayley is about to celebrate her seventeenth birthday is nothing short of a miracle. On that day in September 1999 when our worst fears that Hayley had Hutchinson-Gilford progeria were confirmed, we were told her life expectancy was just thirteen. When I think of other mothers who lost their children before they reached double figures, I realise how blessed we are. Not only do we now understand what causes progeria but there are drugs which seem to be slowing down the rapidly ticking body clocks inside our children.

I know that Hayley finds it a pain having to take so many drugs as part of her daily routine, but it's a small price to pay for more time; even if the results coming out of Boston are not as dramatic as we had first hoped. Hayley hasn't put on weight or grown hair, but you have to be happy with a longer life. The American doctors and scientists have proved that the first trial of the FTI drug Lonafarnib, originally developed to treat cancer, has been the most effective in slowing down progeria. The FTIs act as a barrier to block the harmful molecules that cause progeria. The occasional sickness Hayley suffers as a side effect of taking the drugs is a small price to pay for a healthier body.

All twenty-four of the children who started the trial with Hayley the have seen an improvement in their health and life expectancy. Some, like Hayley, have more flexible blood vessels and stronger bones; others have better hearing and have put on weight. The second and third round of trials which introduced the statin drug Pravastatin, usually used for lowering cholesterol and preventing heart disease, and the bisphosphonate bone drug Zoledronate, usually given to people with osteoporosis, seem to have been less effective. The doctors and scientists think they are working, but they need to analyse the results more before they can say for definite. In the laboratories the scientists have now found a potential cure for progeria in mice. It's a breakthrough, but they are still a long way off proving if it is safe to use on children, so for now Hayley and all the other children taking part in the fourth round of trials will carry on taking the FTIs.

Yet even though I know that Hayley is perfectly fit and well, I can never relax. I'm constantly looking for signs that could mean her health is failing. One morning she woke up coughing. 'Persistent coughing or wheezing can be a sign of heart failure, a result of fluid building up in the lungs,' doctors had warned me.

'Are you OK, chick?' I asked, trying so hard to disguise the panic in my voice.

'Fine, Mum,' came the reply, in her typically not-bothered teenage tone.

It was winter and there were coughs and sniffles doing the rounds. Ruby had the sniffles, so I put it down to a cold. But after a few weeks Hayley was still coughing, I made an appointment to visit our GP.

'It's all right, Mum. I only cough a little bit when I wake up. It doesn't bother me,' she said.

'I don't care, we'll get you checked out,' I insisted.

The doctor listened to her chest and prescribed her a course of antibiotics. But a week later when it still hadn't cleared, they sent her for a chest X-ray. When the doctor scribbled 'Pneumonia?' on her notes, I felt the colour drain from my face. Pneumonia? I knew from my mother's experience of working in an old people's home that a lung infection could be fatal. As the days passed and we waited for the results, I kept looking and listening for signs, telling myself 'no news is good news.'

When the doctor's receptionist called and said the doctor wanted us to book a double appointment to discuss the results, my mind started racing. Pneumonia had claimed the lives of several progeria children over the years. Was this the beginning of the end?

My heart was in my mouth as I took Hayley in to get the results. We walked into the room and there was a strange doctor sitting in place of our usual GP.

'There is nothing of concern in her lungs. But her heart is enlarged,' he said.

I could have kissed him. We already knew the right side of Hayley's heart was larger than the left. Her cardiologist had spotted it during her check-up a couple of years earlier. 'The older we get, the heart has to work that little bit harder,' he had explained, saying it was nothing to worry about. 'Your heart looks perfect; better than mine.'

If the new doctor had compared the X-ray with Hayley's previous ones, he would have realised it was part of her condition. He prescribed a course of antibiotics, but it didn't make any difference. It's still there, but it doesn't seem to bother her. Doctors think it may be caused by some sort of allergy, and she will have to go through many tests before they can pinpoint what is causing it. But as long as pneumonia and heart problems have been ruled out, I feel more relaxed.

Another cause for concern is the inside of her carotid arteries, which carry blood to her brain. A couple of years ago the doctors at Boston Children's Hospital picked up that one of the arteries wasn't flowing properly. During her latest visit the scan showed the other one was also restricted. Naturally this is a worry as carotid artery disease (stenosis) causes strokes, as it stops the blood getting to the brain. It's also worrying that we will have to wait another two years before she goes back to Boston for her next set of checks and scans and anything could happen in that time. The statin drugs and aspirin she takes every day help to reduce the furring inside her arteries; and, if necessary, there is an operation that can be done under local anaesthetic where surgeons can get inside the arteries and take out the fat blocking them, but we don't know whether Hayley would be suitable for such a procedure. Our local Conquest Hospital now has the equipment to carry out these scans. For my own peace of mind I'd like to have it checked out every three months as strokes have claimed the lives of so many progeria children.

The only time I have ever felt like we were going to lose Hayley was when she was told she would never walk again. It was a tough time, having to deal with the loss of her mobility on top of her raging teenage hormones. I watched her change from a bright, bubbly, energetic young girl who loved riding her bike and bouncing on her trampoline to a withdrawn and moody teenager, who just couldn't be bothered with life. Whether it was a symptom of her progeria, or just her age, was hard to know.

Looking back my decision to keep her home from school for almost a year, while we were hoping she would have a hip-replacement operation, was a big mistake. At the time I thought I was doing what was best for her: I wanted to protect her, keep her close and prevent her from being hurt. It was a bad move. She became socially isolated and lost a lot of her friends, to the point where she became awkward around other children her age. She was scared to go out in the wheelchair because she felt that people were looking at her, which has always been the case because she's so well known around the town, but for her the wheelchair was a life-changer.

Even her cardiologist Dr Whincup, who we have always considered to be a friend, noticed the change in her. Months after she had adapted to her new life in a wheelchair, he took me to one side and commented, 'I'm pleased to see she has got the sparkle back in her eyes. I hope you don't mind me saying this but I really thought we were going to lose her.'

I can't begin to imagine how hard it is for her. I have a recurring dream that Hayley walks into my bedroom at night and snuggles up in bed beside me. I so miss the gentle pad of her flat-footed footsteps on the stairs which always told me that Hayley was on her way down to breakfast. Her feet are completely flat, so she always wore slippers around the house to stop them hurting on the hardwood floor. When I was at the kitchen sink up to my elbows in dirty dishwater, she would sneak up on me and make me jump. I always used to shout at her, but now I would give anything to for one more fright.

The network of progeria children in the world is like an extended family, bound together not by blood but by a genetic twist of fate. We share the happy times, support one another through the darker moments, learn about medical breakthroughs and, through the many annual Reunions, we watch the children grow and defy the disease. So whenever a child from our network passes on, it hurts as if it were one of our own family members.

For years all the children in our circle of friends were all happy and healthy. But in recent years we have lost several close friends. Dean Andrews was Europe's oldest survivor of Hutchinson-Gilford progeria. When we first met him, he was twenty and had already surpassed his life expectancy by seven years. He had a girlfriend, a car and tattoos. It was such an inspiration to meet such a bright, fun-loving and funny young man who had never let progeria stand in his way of skateboarding and riding his bike.

While the younger children looked up to him, I became close friends with his mum, Dawn. We would chat regularly over the phone, exchanging news on family life and health scares. But one day in May 2012 Dawn rang to tell me Dean had been taken into a hospice. As a mother, who had connections with our local hospice, I knew it was a bad sign. It could only mean end-of-life care.

'Would you mind if I came to visit him?' I said.

I felt I wanted to be there, I wanted to say goodbye. My instincts were telling me that time was running out.

The children were staying with their dad, Mark, so I jumped in the car and drove for four hours to see the family in Birmingham. When I arrived at the hospice, Dean was lying in bed. He didn't look like the Dean I knew. I kissed the top of his head and whispered 'Are you all right?'

He opened his eyes and I thought I caught the faintest attempt to smile. I held his hand as I passed on good wishes from his friends in Bexhill, and reminded him of the fun times we had at the Reunion.

Driving home I couldn't stop thinking about what Dawn must be going through and prayed he would pull through. The following day I got the call to say he had passed away in the night. His family had been planning his twenty-first birthday, now they had a funeral to plan. Dean had only been part of our 'progeria family' for a short time but it hit us hard. I decided not to go to the funeral; I wanted to remember him as the 'cool guy' sharing his love of music and cars with the younger kids at the Progeria Reunion.

The biggest shock of all was seventeen-year-old Sam Berns. Sam was the reason children like Hayley had been given the chance to live a longer, healthier life. In America, Sam was the face of progeria. When he was diagnosed with progeria at twenty-two months old, his remarkable parents Leslie and Scott had set out to fight the disease head on and founded the Progeria Research Foundation.

Like Hayley, Sam was an incredibly positive and charming young person. His philosophy on life was not to waste energy feeling bad for himself, so he surrounded himself with the people he liked. During our many trips to Boston and holidays in

America, we had grown close to the family and watched Sam develop into a brilliant and wise young man.

When the news reached us from across the Atlantic that Sam had passed away, due to complications from progeria, breaking the news to Hayley, Louis and Ruby was heartbreaking.

Whenever a child passes away Mark and I feel it is our duty as parents to tell Hayley; it would be awful if she found out first on one of her social networks. Telling a seven-year-old child that her best friend had 'gone to sleep and gone to Heaven' was hard. But there is no easy way to tell a sixteen-year-old that her friend who is seventeen and has progeria has passed away. I can't even begin to imagine what goes through her head. She must think, 'I have progeria, I'm sixteen. Am I going to pass away too?' It's almost like she blocks out the bad news. I don't know how she does it. I wish I could be that bullet proof. I know her favourite boy band and that she likes drinking hot chocolate, but I have no idea whether she is scared for the future or resigned to her fate. I feel like I want her to open up and share her worries, but I don't know how to approach such a difficult conversation.

How do you ask your own child what kind of funeral they want?

I have this idea that I'd like to have Hayley's ashes turned into diamonds and made into a necklace, so that I can keep her physically close to my heart forever. I have tried to bring it up in a casual, conversational way.

'Do you remember I told you about my friend whose mother passed away? She's talking about having her Mum's ashes put into ink and having a tattoo,' I said.

'Really? Is that even safe?' she replied.

'I suppose it must be. People do all sorts of things with the ashes of their loved ones these days. I read online that some people have had their ashes made into diamonds and put into rings and necklaces. And in some places you can even have your ashes put into fireworks …'

'I don't like fireworks,' she said, bringing that conversation to an abrupt end.

When her friend Maddie passed away, Hayley said, 'When I go, I want to be buried,' but I can't stand the thought of lowering her

119

into the ground in a box and leaving her there.

I often visit Maddie's grave, especially when I hear 'Chasing Cars' by Snow Patrol on the radio. It was the song playing on the radio after she passed away and the lyrics 'if I lie here, if I just lay here, would you lie with me and just forget the world' broke my heart. In the years after Maddie's passing, Hayley was obsessed with the graveyard, she would nag me to take her to lay letters and gifts and a tiny fairy on the grave to watch over Maddie. But that was when she was seven and had no real concept of death and still called cemeteries gravy yards.

Over the years the plots around Maddie's Piglet-shaped headstone have been filled, but the plot next to her friend has been left untouched. Hayley has stopped visiting the cemetery because it makes her 'too sad' .

'I don't need to go there to remember Maddie, I just think of all the birthdays and sleepovers and fun we had,' she tells me.

Hayley has many playlists of boy bands and punk music on her phone and I too have started my own special playlist. Whenever I hear a song on the radio that has a special meaning or brings back magical memories, I add it to my list. The first one, S Club 7's hit 'Never Had A Dream Come True', reminds me of the farewell party from our last Progeria Reunion in Kent. The nights are always tinged with sadness as we say our goodbyes, never knowing which children will return the following year. As we watched the singer on stage, I held Hayley close and sang along, knowing that as the words of the song said, a part of us would always be together, regardless of where life took us.

'Singing You Through' by All Angels is on my list, too. When I heard it on the radio as I was driving the kids to school, the words jumped out at me.

'Have a listen to the words of this song, aren't they lovely?' I said to Hayley.

'That's really nice,' she said, so I added it to the list along with Kate Bush's 'This Woman's Work'. For me the words, 'Give me these moments back' say it all. All this talk of funeral songs might seem morbid, but I am so scared that when the time comes I won't know what to do, what flowers to choose, what colour coffin to buy or what songs to play. 'Don't tempt fate,' Mark tells me, but I need to have a plan. She loves her music so much, I'm afraid she'll come back and haunt me if I get it wrong.

For now I have to focus on the positive things and plan ahead to make Hayley's life as full and happy as I can. She likes to set me little tasks, to stop me from getting too bored or depressed. Over the years I've organised charity nights, ladies' nights with sexy butlers and male strippers, sponsored leg waxes and summer balls to raise money for Hayley and the Progeria Reunions. Lately she's been hinting that she'd like a summerhouse in the garden, where she and Courtney can chill out in private and listen to music.

When she was a toddler she loved her wooden Wendy house she would spend hours playing in it with Maddie, pretending they were princesses in a castle. Now it just sits empty and unloved at the bottom of the garden, since she and Ruby outgrew it years ago. I've been looking into the summerhouse idea and it's going to cost at least £5,000, so I'm going to have to work hard to raise enough money.

I'm also happy to spend hours online to buy concert tickets for her to see her favourite bands. Her music is all she cares about and at least I know she's doing something she enjoys. I used to think that her Twitter friends and followers were keeping her away from making friends in the real world, but I've now realised that her connections in cyberspace have given her a purpose and a whole new group of friends who have something in common.

With every passing year, she makes me so proud. I still can't quite believe that she has started college when no one ever expected to reach her GCSE year. Yet despite all her hospital appointments and health issues, she worked hard at school, had an excellent attendance record and passed all her exams. As I waved her off on her first day of college, I had flashbacks to the smiling four-year-old in the over-sized blue gingham pinafore dress and navy bandana who set off on her first day at primary school, and I was filled with hope. Her enthusiasm for learning has rubbed off on me and after I dropped her off at college, I decided to go and enrol myself. I've always wanted to be a midwife and I've taken the first steps towards training by starting an Access course. First I have to sit a maths and English exam, but Hayley is happy with that as long as I don't join her class. She's even helping me with my English homework. 'I didn't realise how thick you are,' she keeps telling me whenever I ask her a simple question.

In 2015 we will have the choice of another form of treatment being offered by two of the most important scientists in Spain and France. While the doctors and scientists in America have been working with the FTI drugs that slow down the production of progerin, Dr Carlos López-Otin and Nicolas Lévy at the Marseille-Luminy Centre of Immunology in France have been working on what they call an anti-sense therapy using morpholino drugs that splice the cells and effectively 'turn off' the bad gene that creates progeria.

When we first chose to take part in the trials in Boston, we had the option of taking part in trials in Marseilles, but at the time the scientists were still testing mice and couldn't give us a start date. So we opted to go to America as we didn't have time to waste.

All the parents of progeria children in Europe are being invited to Marseilles to find out more about the new round of trials using the morpholino drugs. I feel as though the clock has been turned back to 2007 and once again we have the difficult task of predicting the future. Should she carry on taking the FTI drugs, which have made such a difference to her health and given her those valuable extra years? Or should she stop taking the FTIs and try the new drugs, not knowing how effective they will be. If she carries on with the FTIs and something happens, will I blame myself for not trying the morpholinos?

It's such a horrible feeling, knowing that the life of your child depends on the decision you make. But ultimately it will be Hayley's decision as she is old enough to make up her own mind; all I can do is present her with all the facts.

People often say to me, 'I don't know how you can be so strong?' It's a mother's natural instinct to protect her young, but until you have to protect your child from a disease that robs them of their youth, you don't realise how strong you can be. I used to think 'What have I done in my life that is so bad that I deserve something like this?' but now I realise what a privilege it is.

Progeria may still be one of the rarest diseases in the world, but the medical research and development that has gone into it in the last ten years has been amazing. When you consider how for many decades scientists have been searching to find cures for other childhood illnesses like cancer and diabetes, yet in the fifteen years since Hayley was diagnosed with progeria, they have found the cause and are working on not one but two treatments. Hayley and all the other special children are providing an insight into the causes of ageing that could change the way we all see old age.

As a parent it fills me with hope that Hayley can go on to celebrate many more birthdays. Already I have big plans for her twenty-first birthday. One day, when she grows out of her obsession with boy bands, I hope she will find someone who loves her as much as I do. I want to be mother of the bride at the world's first progeria wedding. I've always said that Hayley will prove all the doctors wrong and will be the one child with progeria to outlive all life expectancies. No one can ever know how many years they have left, but for now we have to enjoy the moments we have.

Old Before My Time

By Hayley and Kerry Okines with Alison Stokes

Hayley Okines is like no other 13-year-old schoolgirl.

In *Old Before My Time*, Hayley and her mum Kerry reflect on her unusual life. Share Hayley's excitement as she travels the world meeting her pop heroes Kylie, Girls Aloud and Justin Bieber and her sadness as she loses her best friend to the disease at the age of 11.

Now as she passes the age of 13 – the average life expectancy for a child with progeria – Hayley talks frankly about her hopes for the future and her pioneering drug trials in America which could unlock the secrets of ageing for everyone...

For more information about **Hayley Okines**

and other **Accent Press** titles

please visit

www.accentpress.co.uk

For news on Accent Press authors and upcoming titles please visit

http://accenthub.com/

**Find out more about the extraordinary
life of Hayley Okines**

Follow Hayley's blog @ hayleyokines.wordpress.com

facebook.com/OldBeforeMyTime

@ProgeriaBook

**To donate to Hayley's Fund,
please visit Hayley's Progeria Page**

http://hayleyspage.com